The flag on the cover was presented to the author in 1967 by the Air Force upon his promotion to general officer, thus designating him a flag officer

PREVENT
WAR
A New Strategy
for America

by

Jack Kidd
Major General US Air Force (Ret.)

Three Presidents Publishing
P.O. Box 174, Earlysville, Virginia 22936

Published by:
Three Presidents Publishing
P.O. Box 174
Earlysville, VA 22936

Cover Design: Foster and Foster, Inc., Fairfield, Iowa
Editing: Nancy Lang, Commune-a-Key, Salt Lake City, Utah
Typeset Design, Graphics, and Printing: BookMasters, Inc., Mansfield, Ohio

Library of Congress Catalog Card Number
99 097014
ISBN 0-9675786-0-4

Dedication

I dedicate this book to my wife, Amma, who is fully aware of a spouse's first responsibility: help the other to achieve his or her highest calling.

Contents

Acknowledgements

I owe a great deal to those who cheerfully gave invaluable advice, who endeavored to keep me on track, who urged me on when inertia set in, and without which this book would likely never have been printed. To one and all, I thank you.

My wife, Amma, whose contribution sustained me in my endeavors.

C. V. Narasimhan, friend of many years and who was for twenty-three years the Undersecretary-General of the United Nations under three Secretary-Generals, and the author of *United Nations at 50, Recollections,* and many articles.

Benjamin Ferencz, a long-time friend who served as a Chief Prosecutor at the Nuremberg Trials after WW II; was an Adjunct Professor at Pace Law School, where he founded the Peace Center; and most recently has been an ardent advocate of the International Criminal Court Statute, fulfilling a fifty year old dream, and is the author of *Global Survival,* as well as many other books dealing with world peace.

Retired Rear Admiral Eugene Carroll, another friend of many years and a fount of advice and information. For years he has been the Deputy Director of the Center for Defense Information, Washington, D.C.

Norman A. Graebner, Randolph P. Compton Professor Emeritus of History and Public Affairs at the University of Virginia, still active after forty-five years, is the author of *Empire on the Pacific; the New Isolationism; Cold War Diplomacy; Ideas and Diplomacy; The Age of Global Power; America as a World Power, and Foundations of American Foreign Policy.*

Major General (Ret.) Indar Jit Rikhye, Indian Army, Ret., who served in WW II, and had a distinguished career in UN peacekeeping, becoming Military Adviser for Congo Operations to the Secretary-General, author of *Military Adviser to the Secretary General.*

John Woodworth, who worked for years on US foreign and defense policy. He was the deputy negotiator for intermediate-range nuclear forces, with rank of Ambassador; he was the Secretary of Defense representative on delegations to the Conference on Security and Cooperation in Europe; the UN Conference on disarmament; and the US-Soviet INF negotiations in 1981–1983; director of theater nuclear policy in the Pentagon; principal nuclear policy advisor at the US mission to NATO. He holds a Master of Science in Foreign Service degree from Georgetown University and he was a Fellow in Public Affairs at the Woodrow Wilson School, Princeton University. He is currently an Adjunct Faculty member at the Charlottesville, VA. Federal Executive Institute.

Having cited the treasure-trove of knowledge and experience of these renowned individuals, I take full responsibility, nevertheless, for the views and concepts which make up this book

Foreword

I took the road less traveled by—and it made all the difference.

Robert Frost

Why am I writing this book? Because I can't help it. It's a compulsion that won't let me rest.

I see the 20th century being played all over again in the next century unless crucial changes are made. I see few signs that these changes are being identified, much less being implemented.

We close this century with an appalling record, six times deadlier than the last century which holds a record unequaled in history: two world wars, with World War II being the deadliest war ever; three other major wars in which the United States was the major participant. We averaged—from the first to the last—a major war every sixteen years, or in other terms, we were fighting in wars almost 2 days a week for over 73 years. It is significant to note that the United States reacted to the deeds of others in all five of these wars. Altogether 110,000,000 people were killed in these and lesser wars, of which 620,000 were Americans in uniform, and 1,131,000 were wounded. The diversion of resources from productive endeavors and the misery of others affected by war, is incalculable. The cost of the Cold War alone; $13,400,000,000,000 (that's $13.4 trillion), including $4 trillion for nuclear weapons, leaving a debt of over $5 trillion. Even today, at peace, the US spends more than one-third of its budget on the military; also, the US share of global military budgets is one-third.

World War II was precipitated by megalomaniacs Tojo and Hitler; Korea and Vietnam by virulent Communism as spread by other megalomaniacs, Stalin and Mao; the Gulf War by still another, Saddam Hussein; and the Kosovo genocidal operation precipitated by Slobodan Milosevic.

At the beginning of this century no one foresaw the series of wars in which the United States became involved. Preventing not only a repetition of these and lesser wars, but also future wars which will be fought with far deadlier weapons even now on the drawing boards is paramount.

How it happened that I was moved from job to job over 31 years in the US Air Force (and predecessor organizations) and joint staffs and commands, providing me with experience in starting wars, fighting wars, operating wars, planning wars (including World War III) and ending wars, may have something to do with my compulsion. Specifically, I was involved in three of our five major wars this century, World War II, Korea and Vietnam. Had someone set out to prepare me to write this book, he (or she) couldn't have provided me with a better background.

I've been out of uniform for 25 years. A number of these years I was involved in giving about 75 talks from California to Maine and in Moscow twice (at the height of the Cold War) about a plan I devised to end the lose-lose arms race and Cold War with the Soviet Union. It was published in book form in 1988 and is discussed in this book in Part 1, Chapter 10. I have been informed that President Gorbachev received a copy of it. Also our two presidential candidates and every member of congress received a copy.

Since the end of the Cold War and the collapse of Communism I have been watching, waiting for and, yes, writing the White House, the State Department, the Defense Department and members of Congress about taking a leadership role in preventing wars—a role no other nation can provide.

As many readers will be in agreement with the ideas and proposals in this book—and some will be violently opposed—I find it appropriate to say that I am a firm believer in the Constitution of the United States of America (which I have sworn many times to uphold). I note particularly those first words, "We the People . . . " Sometimes we forget that it is we who have the power and we who allow our elected officials to use it on our behalf.

This book is written expressly so every thinking American can understand the issues involved. For those who share the views in this book and who believe that the United States is not doing all it can to prevent war, the book can help coalesce opinion. Recall the many citizen groups that manifested and made their views known during the arms race and the Cold War?

I would be overjoyed if this book spawned a lively debate as to where America is headed, about its leadership role in the world, about not only harnessing weapons of mass destruction as well as eliminating them, about not only reducing the number of wars, but preventing them, and about making the world a safer, saner place.

In this book are the ideas, the motivations—and the plan—to transform the United States into the world leader of a different sort and stature, that will help us achieve the peace that mankind longs for. I propose a New Strategy for America. Now is the time to begin, as by our past experience in this century another war involving the US is due to take place in about the year 2007—unless action is taken now.

Part I

Part One of this book is designed to acquaint you with the author. Some of you are already familiar with my thinking, having heard my talks in the '80s about the lose-lose arms race. I gave about seventy-five talks across the country from California to Maine, and in Moscow. Several millions in that period heard me on radio and TV. Others read my 1988 book, the "Strategic Cooperation Initiative'" which also proposed a way out of the arms race. Note that in 1988 the US-Soviet relationship was still filled with vituperation. Now Russia, a democracy and budding market economy, and the United States cooperate.

All need to know more about my background, my experiences, the way I think and why I think that way, as in Part 2 I propose some rather earthshaking changes to national security policy in our still perilous world. Yes, A New Strategy for America.

1

The Early Days

It all started at age nine, after my parents treated me to a ride in a Curtiss-Robin in 1928. I announced to them right then and there that I was going to be a pilot, an airline pilot. The National Air Races that were held at Glenview, Illinois that year, just north of Chicago and a few miles from my home in Winnetka, had planted the bug in me. Watching those racing planes whizzing around a thirty-mile triangular course, low to the ground, in their vertical banks around the home pylon put the frosting on the cake. I remember that Jimmy Doolittle, later General Doolittle of Tokyo bombing fame, was one of the pilots, flying his snub-nosed Gee-Bee (years later, in England during WW II I had the pleasure of meeting and reminiscing with him). Roscoe Turner was another hero. Those were the days when the Army Air Corps was flying the airmail. The pilots, untrained in instrument flying and flying ill-equipped airplanes, were involved in many crashes. I must have been undaunted by that.

Life for us kids in Winnetka was rather idyllic. It was only a ten minute walk to school. There was the beach at Lake Michigan where we "lived" in the summer—only thirty minutes away on our trusty bikes; and there was Bob Davenport, my best friend and next door neighbor. My bike was a Hibbard, Spencer, Bartlet. One fine day Bob and I set out for the beach. Racing down Snake Hill, the winding road to the beach was always a thrill. But this day, 'flying' down at thirty miles an hour-or-so, a big black sedan rounded the curve and I hit head-on. Had I gone through the windshield I would have been sliced to pieces by that old-fashioned plate glass but instead, I flew over the top of the car, landing on the road well behind it. How I got home I don't remember. I do remember staying on the swing on our front porch for several days, favoring a scraped left foot, the extent of the damage. Then it was back to normal. My bike wasn't. The front and back wheels were squashed together, side-by-side.

Another day Bob and I went swimming, having fun on the pier and diving off. He picked a shallow spot, and hit his head on the bottom. I heard the commotion and ran to help. The lifeguard and several of us helped get him to the beach. The ambulance took forever to reach the Evanston Hospital. I was allowed to ride with him, but then the doctors took over. He had a broken neck and died that night. I lost my best buddy. The impact of that loss has remained with me through the years.

A few words about my parents, both now deceased. Somehow, on a very modest income they managed to settle in the better communities, with the better school systems. First in Winnetka with its touted system (we didn't receive grades, but we carried home a progress chart showing our accomplishments in the various subjects. For some reason we were never taught to write cursive, but to print, which I still do to this day). And then at age fourteen we moved to Lakewood, Ohio, on the lake just west of Cleveland, and then two years later to New Rochelle, New York—'forty-five minutes from Broadway' was the old saw. I was an avid Boy Scout, reaching the next to highest level, Life Scout. Due to the moves I didn't make it to Eagle, the top. My parents' interests centered on their two sons; my brother Bill, five years older, and me. They both came from small towns in Ohio. They were bonded to one another by deep love and respect. As a characterization of their entire relationship I never heard a harsh or spiteful word between them. Only much later did I realize how fortunate I was to have been brought up in such a loving environment.

Dad's name was Caughey, pronounced "Coy," Cleveland Kidd. He headed offices for the Cleveland-based Upson-Walton Company, originally chandlers to the large cargo-carrying sailing ships on the Great Lakes. Wire and manila rope became their main products later. Dad used to take me with him on his business trips. On one we went deep into a coal mine. He was a great handyman, some of which rubbed off on me.

Mom, Hazel Margia Maskey Kidd, was a great mother and the typical housewife, in the times of the '30s. In those depression days no middle class wife with children had a job outside the home. Her home life was her job, which she did superbly. I am reminded that her brother, Carl, was the family genealogist, having put together a family tree dating back to the early 1700s. My son John, is now the keeper of the family tree. Mom was a very devout woman and very private in her spirituality. We followed the practice in our home wherein faith healed, making materia medica and prescription drugs unnecessary. This abiding faith in my health and sense of well-being has stuck with me ever since, though now I do get annual checkups.

I was nineteen before I saw a doctor; he was a US Army Air Corps flight surgeon. I had decided that the Army Air Corps was the best route to becoming an airline pilot. In fact, I failed the first examination for Flying Cadet. My visual depth perception—which had to do with judging the distance above the ground in landing an airplane—was outside the limit. I worked for weeks exercising the eye muscles under the supervision of an optometrist. That summer, as a counselor at Camp Lakewood, a boys camp near Chelsea, Michigan, I received permission from the University of Michigan to measure the depth perception tester, a contraption with two strings attached to two small black posts inside a lighted box. After lining up those two posts on my mockup all summer and fall, it was "No Problem" at the next physical exam.

That summer I bought my first car for $10. I think the fact that the girl I was "gaga" about was the niece of the dealer had a bit to do with the price. It was an ancient Model T Ford coupe, with three pedals on the floor and stage coach door handles. After the campers were bedded down it was great fun to go frog hunting at night, hauling up to twelve friends in and on the car. Those cars didn't have fuel pumps, so on a steep hill they had to be turned around and backed up the hill. At the end of the summer I sold it to a junk dealer in Oberlin, Ohio, my college town, for $5. Rather cheap transportation! And with gas at eight cents a gallon.

Speaking of my college days at Oberlin, a few comments to highlight the contrasts in society, then and now. One of my college classmates was thrown out of college for drinking one glass of whiskey. The word "drugs" was unknown, there simply weren't any. And there was the story that an incoming eighteen year old freshman girl didn't know how babies were born. Sex, as experienced today, was virtually unknown. And I had to sell the car because students weren't allowed to have them.

I decided to leave Oberlin College in the middle of my junior year to become a Flying Cadet, having put in the required two years of college. In retrospect, "put in" is an apt description as I simply went through the motions of getting an education. And wouldn't you know, that once enlisted as a Flying Cadet in the Army Air Corps in Columbus, Ohio in February, 1940 it was back to the airfield at Glenview, Illinois Airfield, the very airfield where my dreams of flying were first conceived. To pinpoint the era, it was the night before the physical exam that I saw the new release, "Gone With the Wind," at a local Columbus theater. In those days the Air Corps was 50,000 strong, with about 2300 aircraft. Five years later it would be 2,500,000 strong with over 78,000 aircraft, even after the severe attrition of WW ll.

Small anecdote. I had planned to take an airline flight from Cleveland to Columbus to be enlisted, but was informed the weather had forced cancellation of the flight. So a friend, Gordy Bennett, with whom I still keep in touch, dropped me off at the Waterloo train station, a few miles south of Oberlin. Upon boarding I went to the dining car, seating myself in the last available seat, opposite a man in an American Airlines uniform. After a few words it turned out that he was to have been the pilot on my canceled flight. What a wonderful talk about the Air Corps and his experiences in it and his airline flying—all the way to Columbus. His name I remember to this day: Captain Fuzzy Robinson. We bumped into each other again at La Guardia Airport years later.

Parenthetically, I've wondered ever since why a Primary Flying School was located at Glenview, Illinois, for when the class of twenty students arrived in February we were flying in zero degree weather, in an open cockpit PT-13 biplane, learning to land on a snow-covered grass field. We looked like WW I pilots with helmet, goggles, sheepskin suits and, of course, the streaming white silk scarf. There was a plus, though, for when the temperature was frigid on a Saturday, drilling was canceled; we were tickled that we could leave for town earlier. I'm sure the drill sergeant wasn't put out.

From there it was on to basic and advanced flying schools at Randolph and Kelly bases near San Antonio. On October 4, 1940 I pinned on Second Lieutenant bars and received the rating of pilot the next day. That same day I received five students. It was student one day and instructor the next. My boss was First Lieutenant Jack Ryan (we didn't address our superiors by their first name) who looked after five instructor of which I was one. (After Kelly Field I was to meet him nearly thirty years later, in his office in the Pentagon, which carried the sign "Chief of Staff, United States Air Force" on his door).

After graduating eight classes of five students it was off to B-17 pilot training School at Sebring, Florida in the spring of 1942 to become a Flying Fortress pilot. This was a few months after Pearl Harbor. Some of our training missions were devoted to looking for German submarines off the coast of Florida. We didn't see any. My brother had become a Navy pilot and was stationed at several bases up and down the East Coast throughout the war, also looking for German subs in his PBYs. I took a ride with him once, taking the wheel of a flying boat for the first and only time. Sebring was my grandmother's (Lonie L. Getter) home, with whom I spent some wonderful hours. She was feisty, even in her '80s. One of her favorite sayings: "Beer is the Devil's own urine."

In October, 1942 the order was cut creating the 100th Bomb Group (Heavy). It was Captain Kidd, Squadron Commander, soon to have 12 B-17s and 350 men assigned. Thus began our training period, preparing for combat. For the next few months it was from pillar to post, or more accurately, moving airplanes and people from Boise, Idaho to Walla Walla, Washington, to Wendover, Utah (at the west end of the Great Salt Lake, quite like at the end of the earth), to Sioux City, Iowa, to Kearney, Nebraska, all in seven months. Mary Jane, my first wife, and the other wives became expert at ferreting out motels. In Wendover we lived in the back of the only structure in town, a gas station.

At Sioux City it was so cold that the water in the toilet froze over in the motel. One night I was on duty as the Group Control officer for cross country navigation training flights. A check at the weather office manned by Lt. Clif Frye verified the awful weather outside: 25 mile-an-hour gusting wind, blowing snow, 25 degrees below zero, making the chill factor about minus 75 degrees. The forecast was for more of the same. I called off flying, went to my room on base and went to sleep. About 10 P.M. there was a knock at the door. I opened to our group commander who had been downtown to dinner at another officer's quarters. He asked, "Why aren't the airplanes flying?" I explained the weather situation to him. His response, "Get 'em in the air." Perplexed, I said, "Yes, sir."

I dressed and returned to the weather office. The weather was unchanged. No change in the forecast either. Our regular procedure in cold weather was to, in effect, erect a tent over each engine, start a fire below it to generate enough heat so that the airplane's starter could turn the engine over sufficiently to run. Frostbite was a risk to the mechanics who worked outside.

I decided to take no action and to accept the responsibility, so I returned to my room and again went to sleep. Next morning I awaited my fate. Nothing. Not a word. It's the only time, ever, that I disobeyed a direct order of my superior officer.

Not long after, the Group Commander was relieved of his duty, but on different grounds.

From Kearney, Nebraska, where the group completed training, it was off to the war. Enroute I detoured just a bit to buzz my college town, Oberlin, dropping to about 500 feet, with all four propellers revved up, making quite a racket. A few days later all twelve of my squadron's airplanes arrived in England.

2

World War ll

After training was completed, our 48 aircraft and crews headed across the Atlantic in May, 1943. On arrival at our new base at Thorpe Abbots in East Anglia, England it was then Major Kidd, the first Group Operations Officer, under our third Group Commander. My new assignment placed me as third in the chain of command of the Group at age 24. My duties were to organize the bombing missions of the group; to brief each mission; to oversee group air training, navigation, bombing; and to serve as command pilot leading bombing missions—in short, to make the biggest possible dent on the enemy.

The modus operandi was to fly in a Group formation of 21 aircraft, a Wing of 63 aircraft and a Division of multiple wings. The Group formation was the basic unit on most missions; it took up airspace of about 1000 feet vertically and about 2000 feet horizontally, devised for protection from enemy fighters and flak, as well as with bombing patterns in mind. No two aircraft were at the same level. Groups bombed individually, separating at an "Initial Point" for the bombing run, then regaining the wing formation. Wings, as well as Divisions, followed each other in trail, all taking up an enormous amount of airspace, normally flying between 20,000 to 28,000 feet (almost five miles high). To the enemy population on the ground it must have been a frightful sight, wondering if the bombs were meant for them, particularly when contrails were formed which became long tubes of cloud visible at great distances.

I normally led the Group or the Wing, but did lead General LeMay's 3rd Air Division once—as a twenty-four year old Lieutenant Colonel—to a major target in Germany, Berlin. (I went from college junior to Lt. Colonel in three and one-half years). On that mission only one aircraft out of over 180, was lost thanks to an undercast, and in spite of the radar directed firing of 800 to 1000 heavy anti-aircraft guns ringing Berlin. We were then bombing using a new radar in the lead aircraft and also, employing another new invention, chaff (packets of aluminum strips about 12 inches long), scattered over the target by the faster Royal Air Force Mosquito's. The chaff was designed to confuse the radars of the otherwise lethal anti-aircraft artillery. It worked well.

How did I feel about bombing a city? By this stage of the war many cities had been bombed, after Germany started the heinous practice by bombing the small town of Coventry, in England. We were inured. It had to be done. Get the war over quicker, the sooner the better. Thinking back on it, it's a horrendous thing to do, but that's war. It's that trait in the human character, or should I say in the character of some humans, to try to achieve their ends no matter what the cost. I refer to Hitler, of course. I trust that what follows in this book just might prevent a repetition of such conduct—by changing the system—as well as reducing and one day eliminating, the instance of war.

Other missions were not as fortunate as that Berlin mission. On August 17, 1943 I led the last and low group of then Colonel LeMay's Division. I think that was the last mission he flew. His boss, General Spaats, Eighth Air Force Commander, grounded him. He was too valuable. Good judgment, as General LeMay became head of the Strategic Air Command and later, Chief of Staff of the Air Force.

This was a unique shuttle mission, bombing the Messersmitt aircraft plant at Regensburg in Bavaria and then continuing on across the tip of Italy where a single anti-aircraft round exploded near us over Lake Garda, then across the Mediterranean to Algeria, where we landed on the gravelly open desert near Telergma.

The Luftwaffe's tactics at that time were to overtake the bomber stream, then turn and make head-on attack on the bombers and we, as tail-end-Charley—the last Group—bore the brunt of the attack in spite of the 11 .50 caliber machine guns firing 600 rounds a minute from each airplane or the 231 guns in our 21 aircraft formation with which we took our toll of German fighters. I didn't envy the German fighter pilots having to fly through our withering fire. We lost 9 of our 21 airplanes and 90 men that day, one aircraft having ditched in

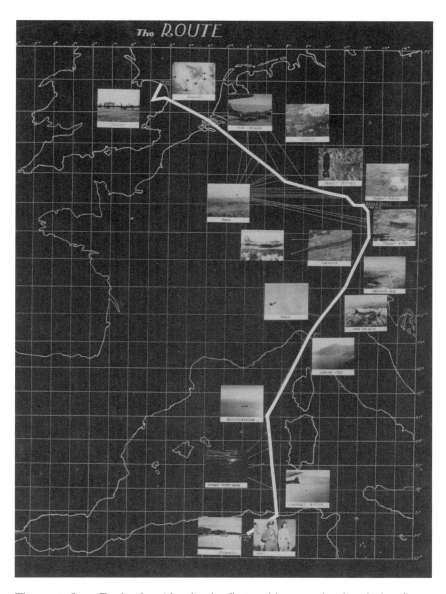

The route from England to Algeria: the first and longest shuttle mission flown by the group.

Lake Lucerne in Switzerland, with the crew spending the rest of the war there due to its neutral status.

At the de-briefing Colonel LeMay asked me where the rest of my airplanes were. My reply was "shot down." That ended the conversation.

Regensburg was one of the two targets that day, Schweinfurt the other. Altogether 376 bombers were dispatched by the 8th Air Force, and 60 were lost. The reason for the shuttle to North Africa was to minimize losses by not flying back through the German defenses; had we retraced our route I think the casualties would have been significantly higher.

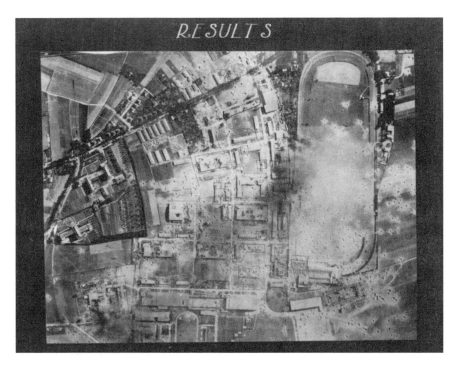

The target, a Messerschmit Me-109 fighter aircraft factory, was obliterated minutes after the attack.

Several days later on our way back to the UK, having refueled our 1,600 gallon tanks by hand pumps from 55 gallon drums and rearmed our own airplanes, we bombed the airport at Bordeaux, a launching base for German aircraft during the war in the Atlantic period.

A week's vacation in North Africa

A week's vacation in North Africa (*continued*)

Months later the 100th flew another shuttle mission to Russia bombing targets both coming and going. On the ground in Russia our aircraft were the target, bombed by German aircraft the first night in Russia, as the Russian defenses were unable to cope. Thankfully, no aircraft or crew members were lost. The crew members took to foxholes—for the only time in the war.

As an aside, in 1994 the US and the USSR were allied, coordinating American operations against Germany. Ironically, only a few short years later we were dire enemies.

Another unforgettable mission was to Bremen. I say "unforgettable" because the details of this and other missions involving enemy action are still etched into the memory bank. On October 8, 1943 the target was the submarine yards, which impacted the war in the Atlantic Ocean. That day I was leading the 13th Combat Wing of 63 Forts (B-17s). At the IP (Initial Point), where we separated to bomb the target by groups. The azure sky was black with flak from the anti-aircraft fire against earlier groups over the target. The most earnest prayer I can recall was offered in those moments. The toughest job I've ever had to do as command pilot was to do nothing on the 10 to

12 minute bomb run—until bombs-away. There was nothing to do but keep quiet on the intercom so as not to distract the bombardier. The bombardier, Capt. Jim Douglass, was actually flying the airplane with his bombsight. Imagine the pressure he was under. Captain Ev Blakely, the pilot and Capt. Harry Crosby, the navigator, similarly sat on their hands. The one saving grace was that no German fighter planes were near at the moment. They avoided their own flak.

It's as vivid today as it was almost sixty years ago. Just at 'bombs away' our aircraft 'jumped' from the explosion under us. There was no doubt the German gunners almost five miles below had used their box barrage technique against our formation, which consisted of 16 88mm ack-ack guns which threw up 25 lb. shells designed to fill with flak the cube of airspace that our 21 aircraft filled; the shells burst at a preset altitude, sending shards of shrapnel in all directions. When they hit the skin of the aircraft it sounded like rice thrown at the car of the bride and groom driving off after the wedding. Our 'rice' was of a far deadlier kind.

This day they did well. Just as bombs were away they box-barraged us squarely, for in an instant eight of our 21 aircraft were knocked out of formation, seven of which didn't make it back to base. In my airplane it was instant fire in the number three engine, the propeller dome on number four engine punctured, the crankshaft broken, leaving us with a windmilling propeller on the far right which set up a drag on the right side of the airplane. Our only power was from engines 1 and 2, on the left side, the number three propeller having been feathered (aligned with the air flow). With only two engines there was only one way to go. Down. And all by ourselves. What was left of the group was scattered. The wing had no leader. Our normal airspeed was about 225 mph, incredulously slow compared to modern aircraft. But now, perforce, we settled for about 95 mph, not far above stalling speed (stalling involves loss of control of the aircraft, resulting in spinning downward toward the ground).

Out of the flak, came German fighters which again swarmed for the kill, sniping at our airplane all the way to Holland. Our gunners claimed 12 shot down; they were officially awarded 9, a record from a single bomber I believe, for the entire air war in Europe.

It was down to 3000 feet over Holland where we could see the muzzle flashes as the enemy took their last shots at us. I grabbed the controls to turn left, while at the same time the pilot, Captain Everett

Blakely, was trying to turn to the right. I recall, uttering an expletive, adding "let's go one way or the other." Over water, everything of any weight went over the side, gun barrels, ammunition, and the bomb-sight, a scarce new self-erecting type. Soon we were able to level off and maintain an altitude—at 950 feet above the North Sea—with full power on our two left Curtiss-Wright engines (the engines and air-planes were marvels of reliability in those days. And the marvel of self-sealing fuel tanks brought many a wounded airplane back to home base). Had we ditched into the drink we'd have been goners, as we found out later that our two life rafts were shredded—as was the skin of our airplane. The North Sea water frigid and rescue air-craft wouldn't likely venture into enemy controlled waters.

As we limped toward the coast of England at about 90 mph, canted about 15 degrees to the left to hold direction, we used the sun for a compass. Thankfully, we were able to transfer fuel from the right to the left wing tanks. We landed at the first airfield sighted, only to find it was a dummy field, with dummy aircraft, designed to attract enemy attack. We lowered the landing gear on final approach, but when the wheels hit the runway, the rudder cable snapped, the tail wheel didn't extend. We hit the engine switches to prevent a fire, the wind milling prop flew off its hub and, almost like a Hollywood script, with no control we headed for the only two trees on the "air-field." Of course, we hit the largest of the two head-on, an ancient oak, literally wiping the nose off the airplane. I can still hear the bro-ken oxygen lines hissing. Another miracle. We didn't catch fire. My first inclination was to slide out the copilot's window which was about ten feet above the ground, risking a landing on my head. Luck-ily it was just too small. Then it dawned on me that in our new cir-cumstances I could just walk out the nose of the airplane, with a short jump to the ground.

Our wounded were carried to the ground. We dispatched the able crew members to seek help. It was a wonder that no one was curious enough to come in our direction. It seemed hours before help arrived to take the four wounded to the hospital in Norwich. Later we learned that Sgt. Saunders died of his wounds that night.

Interestingly, I have no recollection of how we covered the 30-40 miles to our base, or how we were received. Joyously, I'm sure. By the time of our arrival the intelligence debriefing would

The end of a long day's work

The end of a long day's work (*continued*)

have already painted the Group Commander a clear picture of the day's events. I still don't know who gathered our fourteen surviving aircraft together and led them home—much less the other two groups.

For months after returning to the US in the fall of 1944 I had nightmares about these two missions. But now, in writing about the Bremen mission, I got to thinking even deeper into the possibilities we faced.

We'd have been in even *deeper trouble* than we were in already if:

1. The ack-ack round had burst a few feet closer to the airplane.
2. The windmilling propeller on engine #4 had left its hub and come through the cockpit.
3. The fire in the #3 engine nacelle persisted.
4. The small arms fire from the ground in Holland been more accurate.

5. One of the two engines operating at full throttle had sputtered over land.
6. Our gunners had not done such an outstanding job in defending us.

We'd *all have been done in for sure* if just one of the following had occurred:

1. The ack-ack round exploded inside the airplane.
2. One of the two operating engines even sputtered over the icy North Sea, as the life rafts were shredded, the fuselage punctured with hundreds of holes.
3. The necessary fuel could not have been transferred from the right wing to the left, resulting in fuel starvation over the North Sea.
4. Had the rudder cable snapped over water or close to the ground, instead of upon touching the runway on landing, as it did.

Don't think that prayers are not heard.

It just so happened that I flew both these missions with the same crew, the pilot, Ev Blakely, who is now retired in California, the navigator; Harry Crosby, who became the 8th Air Force navigator and is a retired Professor of English from Boston College, now living in Maine; Jim Douglass, the bombardier, and Lt. Charley Via, the co-pilot, who had the dubious honor of manning the tail guns—where my presence as Command Pilot placed him to be my eyes from that vantage point. And of course the gunners who defended us nobly and who contributed the most "kills," setting that American record of enemy fighters shot down by a bomber in Europe.

I'll recount just one more mission. To be accurate, it was a "nonmission," but I include it because it sheds a bit of light on the character of General LeMay.

The target was an oil refinery in northwest Germany (I've forgotten its name, which will be immaterial, as you will soon see). The mission was unique in that it set up a feint, designed to flush the German fighters when they were refueling on the ground, to attack. The planned flight route called for heading toward the coast of Germany, then turning to the northeast, then north, then west, and then south, crossing the coast—in other words, flying a rectangle large enough to exhaust the fighters' fuel, then attack.

There was only one problem: weather. On the first leg, heading toward Denmark, we ran into flat banks of stratus clouds. As large formations must change course and altitude slowly, individual aircraft left the formation for safety reasons. Scattered would probably be a more accurate word. I recall that I could see only one other aircraft, the visibility about 100 feet. Upon breaking out into clear air, the copilot—my eyes to the rear in the tail gun position—reported many stragglers, which he said were closing in on our group. Moments later he reported that aircraft from five different groups were following us like a gaggle of geese. It was a tribute to the 100th group discipline that it remained intact. As the command pilot I was stuck with making a decision. The factors zipped through my mind: would we run into the clouds again, and what kind of bombing pattern could be achieved. I decided to abort, to head for home base.

I don't recall when I began to think of the consequences of my decision. We simply didn't abort. It was not in General LeMay's nature. In fact, a rule had been adopted that if a gunner became ill while still forming over England he would bail out, the aircraft going on to target. Several did bail out, getting back to base hours later.

After returning to base and the usual debriefing, Colonel Harding, the Group C.O. (Commanding Officer) told me that there would be a critique of the mission at now General LeMay's 3rd Division Headquarters the next day. I didn't sleep well that night. At the end of the discourse General LeMay set the policy: missions would be aborted when formation integrity could not be maintained. He reasoned that the standard formation was designed to provide maximum firepower against attacking aircraft—as well as provide the best bombing pattern and defense against antiaircraft fire.

What a relief! To the best of my knowledge no formation leader ever had to abort a mission thereafter.

What does this stress do to a man? Having put in probably more than thirty twenty-four hour stints on the job and a dozen or so thirty-six hour stints without sleep, I went from 180 pounds to 140 pounds. Toward the end of my sixteen months, every time I passed through the 10,000 foot level, I got excruciating tooth aches, my gums having pulled away from the teeth. My gums were like an altimeter. I knew when we climbed through the 10 thousand foot level.

Many books have recounted those days: "A Wing and A Prayer," by Harry Crosby, the Group Navigator, wrote about the 100th Bomb Group; "The Schweinfurt-Regensburg Mission," by Martin Middlebrook; "Double Strike" and "Flying Fortress" by Jablonski; "Courage, Honor and Victory" by Ian Hawkins; and "The Mighty Eighth," by Gerald Astor.

All in all I was in the same job of Group Operations Officer for 16 months before heading home to the ZI (Zone of the Interior, or US). I had served under seven Group Commanders since the order was cut 22 months earlier creating the Group. One, Colonel Kelly, lasted one week. He was shot down a few miles inside the French coast opposite England on a No Ball mission, bombing the sites from which buzz bombs were launched to attack London. Capt. Summer Reeder and I were the last two original pilots to leave the Group in August, 1944. Sadly, he was killed soon after returning to the US, hit by a microburst—a severe vertical wind—while taking off in a C-54 transport.

In those 16 months the 100th flew 216 missions. I led 18 of them. We lost 176 aircraft to flak and fighters, which amounted to 360 percent the authorized strength (48) of a bomb group; 1,456 men were lost, representing 300 percent of authorized strength (480), and the 581 killed or missing in action, 121 percent. The difference between aircraft lost and crew members lost can be attributed to the likes of Lt. Rosy (Robert) Rosenthal (later Lt. Colonel) whose crew bailed out into the midst of a tank battle east of Berlin. Thankfully, he and his crew were picked up by the Russians. They were taken to Moscow, feted by Ambassador Harriman, returning to the 100th by way of Spain. He was shot down again in France, breaking an arm in the crash landing and again returned to the group to fly many more missions. About fifty I think, more than any other pilot. He simply would not quit, flying more than the prescribed number of missions, which in the early days was 25. He became a lawyer in New York and is now retired in Mamaroneck, NY.

Our worst one day loss was 12, two days after the Bremen mission. The target was Peenemunde where Germany's V-2 missiles were made. We had only 13 airplanes due to attrition. Only one came

Goodbye, after 16 months of war. Left to right. Rosy Rosenthal, Tom Jeffrey, the new group commander, Sumner Reeder, and Sammy Barr.

back. The 100th was flat on its back—but with the same spirit and determination that motivated all the members of the Group throughout, it rejuvenated quickly, maintaining that spirit right through to the end of the war.

In the entire 16 months of my tour of duty only one individual shirked his duty, a pilot who claimed he couldn't be responsible for his crew. The remainder of our normal 5000-man strength of the group met every challenge, in the air and on the ground. It was young Americans at their best.

I didn't envy those who hit the beaches on D-Day. Their toll was tremendous. We flew 77 sorties, some crews flying two missions on D-Day in direct support of the invasion. But from my perspective it was D-Day every time we went out on a mission.

General Eisenhower paid all of us who fought the air war, including the RAF, a tribute in his Original Invasion Orders: "Our air offensive [against Germany] has seriously reduced their strength in the air and their capacity to wage war on the ground."

3

INTERLUDE

Back home to see the wife, Mary Jane. We were married a few months before departing for overseas, and were together only about a third as long as I was overseas. After a second honeymoon it was Santa Monica to await reassignment. When it came, it was to the Pentagon. The prospect of working in such a confined space didn't send me. It was a train trip all the way. I expressed my views on arrival and got agreement that if I could clear with Operation, Plans, and Personnel I could go back to California. I did—and in retrospect, this was a mistake—which will become obvious. Back to Santa Monica.

Soon the firm assignment came. To Nellis AFB at Las Vegas, as the Director of Operations of the Air Force Flexible Gunnery School, training gunners for B-17 and B-24 aircraft.

At the end of the war I realized my childhood dream by joining Western Airlines as a copilot in January 1946. The pay was $220 a month, a two-thirds drop in pay—and with a wife and a young son. After three years of flying all their routes, including their LA-Denver route in unpressurized DC-4s over the Rocky Mountains and their two other models, the DC-3 and the Convair 240, I decided that airline flying was not for me. Too akin to a bus driver. My apologies to all the many fine airline pilots.

My son John is now a retired Air Force pilot with wife, Robyn, and three kids, one in business and two in college, and now teaches pilots on the new Air Force C-17 cargo plane. My daughter, Laurie, and her husband, Joe, have two great young girls and both operate thriving businesses.

So, back into uniform. I was ordered directly from Culver City, California to Hq. Combined Airlift Task Force in Wiesbaden,

Germany, Commanded by Major General William Tunner. That was my first time in Germany—on the ground. They pinned the title of Chief, Flight Operations on me. My main job, was the maximizing of the flow of food and coal to the beleaguered citizens in Berlin, then surrounded by the Soviet Army; I did pilot trips occasionally. Early on the pattern was refined to fly C-47s and DC-4s at a three minute separation, day, night and in all weather from Wiesbaden and Rhine Main air bases to the Tempelhof airdrome and return, shutting down traffic only when weather actually went below landing minimums in Berlin. This meant returning the stream of traffic in the air pipeline back to base. This policy was maintained in order to get the maximum tonnage to Berlin. A critical task was making the judgment call as to when to restart the flow, having to estimate one and one-half hours in advance as to when the ceiling and visibility would reach instrument landing requirements in Berlin. Some may recall seeing a movie which pictured the planes descending between apartments in a complex where the pilots could actually see people eating at the dining table.

The British and French air lifts flew their own routes into their own air bases in Berlin.

On April 15, 1950, my birthday, General Tunner put on a maximum effort, flying 15,000 tons in twenty-four hours to Berlin. It gave me a great deal of satisfaction to be a participant in this humanitarian effort, to help the German people get back on their feet, after having a hand in turning Berlin into rubble.

The remainder of my tour in Germany was as a troop carrier Squadron Commander and Group Operations officer, involved with US and French paratroopers.

Air Force pilots log flying hours either as a primary duty or on proficiency flights away from a desk job. My last primary military cockpit duty was in 1942, and from then on my primary job was behind a desk, except for flying in a command pilot role in combat. Altogether I accumulated about 7500 hours in the air, including the airline time, which equates to 10 1/2 months in the air.

4

The Pentagon

My first of three tours in the Pentagon started in 1952. It turned out to be a four year stint. In one step it was like being pulled out of the assembly line of a small company and suddenly being placed in the CEO's office of a mammoth company as an executive, a totally new and fascinating world. What a challenge, to be thrust into a building with 30,000 employees, especially when the military expects one to figure out virtually overnight how the whole process works—and expects results almost instantly. This is a good time to interject that in military service, one is reassigned every 2–4 years, placed into twenty-or-so totally new assignments (businesses) in one career and expected to improve the bottom line instantly in each, to use a business analogy. The very process sharpens one's skills in sizing up situations, and to make positive contributions to each new organization's mission.

My views about the Pentagon changed rapidly. The beginning hodgepodge soon changed to a very logical, organized system. Fortunately, because there were to be two more tours—10 years altogether in the Pentagon. The first tour was an assignment to the Joint Plans Branch of the Directorate of Plans, Air Staff, right in the thick of things, working on the Army-Navy-Air Force war plans, the national contingency war plans and the World War III war plan vis-a-vis the Soviet Union. My initial assignment was that of working the Far East-Pacific national contingency war plans, of which there were several. The immediate nagging issue, though, was the on-going war in Korea. At the time of my arrival the focus was on finding ways to end it, sending briefs up the line to the Chief of the Air Force on any inspirations we had. I recall a Sunday afternoon when three of us had our heads together brainstorming solutions in an almost empty Pentagon. The door opened and the Chief of the Air Force, "Tommy" White, poked his head in and inquired what we were doing. I filled him in quickly. He smiled and left. He received our handiwork the next day. He was a fine gentleman. As of this writing the Korean War continues, as a peace treaty has never been signed.

After struggling to master the formulating and writing of legal-like briefs on war plans and related issues recommending positions on issues for the Chief of the Air Force for his meetings with the Joint Chiefs of Staff, it was like being a duck in water. At this kind of formal planning I was a natural. I found, though, that not everyone has a bent for planning. And war planning was a bit tough on family life; I estimated that in four years I put in about 25% overtime, generated in large measure by the rigid JCS agendas. It became almost a given that at five minutes to five on a Friday afternoon the phone would ring with the message, "JCS paper XYZ is on Monday's agenda." The meetings were normally held at 0900 on Monday, Wednesday and Friday. The poor secretaries! One Saturday morning our three-year-old daughter climbed into bed with us. When she heard that I was going to the Pentagon she said, "You go to that G . . . D . . . Pentagon all the time." I deny any knowledge as to the origin of those words.

The formal procedures for briefing the Chief of the Air Force involved preparing the initial written brief, then on the more important issues orally briefing up the line as necessary: the Director of Plans; the Deputy Chief of Staff, Operations; and the Chief himself. Frequently on the more important issues we—the action officers—were debriefed at the appropriate level to keep us abreast of developments, providing continuity for follow-on actions. In one of the briefings for Major General Herb Thatcher, Director of Plans, labeled me the "idea man," an appellation I've silently savored all these years. By listening to fellow briefers at these sessions the broader pattern soon emerged. The same general practice applied to the meetings of the Joint Planners, usually the two-star level. Likewise, we staffers briefed them and were debriefed by them. Of course the written and oral briefings were all security classified as was most of our work, which was almost always Secret or Top Secret. In view of the broad nature and the high security classification of issues and the fact that as planners we were responsible for planning and briefing issues in all areas across the Air Staff: operations, logistics, communications, not to mention the reading of classified State Department message traffic, we planners were required to have a special security clearance.

When I arrived there were two Unified Commanders in the Pacific Ocean area, Commander-in-Chief, Far East, CINCFE, based in Japan and CINCPAC, based in Hawaii, responsible for the remainder of the Pacific. Every time forces were moved from one area to another it required a formal JCS approval. I pointed out so many times in the briefs to Chief the inefficiency of having two Unified Commands in the Pacific that I feel I had a hand in creating the single Unified Commander for the entire Pacific, with Sub-Unified Commanders reporting to him. ("Unified" translates to "all services"). It remains that way today.

One day I was told by the Director of Plans that, as of that moment I was responsible for reconnaissance matters, a super-sensitive area, so sensitive that I was instructed to skip two bosses to hold those with need-to-know to a minimum, a rather tricky position to be in. A time came when I was asked to coordinate a JCS-approved reconnaissance operation with the Director of the CIA and the Secretary of State—yes, I was a lieutenant colonel. The meeting went well and quickly with Allen Dulles. He asked me what I wanted him to do. I said, "Please initial here." He did, and I departed. At State it was a little different. I made an appointment to meet with the Secretary. When I arrived in the Pentagon-supplied staff car the "horse holders" (a title some of us used for those staff people supporting and surrounding a notable official) let me know in a most diplomatic way that the Secretary wasn't about to meet with a lieutenant colonel. So the next day I returned with Major General Dick Lindsay, Air Force Director of Plans. We were admitted (the Secretary was out of town so we met with the Deputy, Herbert Hoover, Jr.). We transacted our business and left.

Later, General Lindsay took a couple of us with him in a C-54 on a visit to all the principal Air Force Commands in the Pacific, Alaska. Japan, Korea, Okinawa, Taiwan, Hawaii and the Philippines. Very educational, having been briefed by all the commands.

One day I was ordered to deliver some papers to the 5th Air Force Intelligence Officer. I'd never been a courier before or since.

With a metal-lined valise handcuffed to my wrist I headed for Japan in an Air Force transport airplane. The valise was placed in the proper hands. Of course, I wondered what was in it. And why the information wasn't sent by Top Secret message, as our communications were known to be secure. Years later I read in the newspaper that President Eisenhower had considered using the atomic bomb on North Korea. The contents of my case must have been the targets.

At the end of the third year, taking over from Colonel Lucius Clay, Jr., the son of General Clay, and himself later a general, I was made Chief of the Joint War Plans Branch, thus getting immersed in all the war plans including the WW III plan.

In the early days of nuclear weapons the Air Force was allocated the great preponderance of them, most going to the Strategic Air Command. It was the period when the Soviets were in the early stages of their tremendous buildup which would mirror our force posture: the thermonuclear weapon; the intercontinental bomber and ballistic missile; the missile submarine. None of this set off any alarm bells for me. The United States was paramount. We were on the right track. I foresaw no problems.

Then, I was off to the Air War College at Maxwell Air Force Base at Montgomery, Alabama. It was a welcome change from the hectic pace of the Pentagon. Lots of lectures. A few papers to write. It was a broadening experience. For some reason I remember one guest professor saying that the day interest rates in the US ever got to 10% the economy would collapse. What year was it that the prime rate got to near 20%?

It was there that I was promoted to Colonel.

This nine months brought my college level credits in effect to about 3 1/2 years. In all I've received credits from seven institutions of higher learning, including Oberlin College, the University of San Antonio, the University of New Mexico, and the University of Maryland campuses in Germany and the Pentagon. I'm still 'working' on a college degree.

5

GETTING ACQUAINTED
WITH NUKES

One never knew what to expect in a new assignment. This one had me wondering. I was off to the Air Force Special (Nuclear) Weapons Center (AFSWC) in Albuquerque, New Mexico in June, 1957 as the Director of Operations (DO). The function of the DO was to coordinate the functions of the Center: research, development and test, all new to me. Research focused on the effects of nuclear blasts, for example, the impact on structures, such as missile silos, as well as blast and radiation effects on humans. The development and engineering section worked with the airframe contractors to the Air Force and the Atomic Energy Laboratories, acting as a middleman to fit nuclear weapons to Air Force weapons systems, such as the B-52s. Test did just that. It participated in nuclear tests in Nevada and at Bikini/Eniwetok. The 4950th Test Group, equipped with the British made B-57 bomber was noted for its high altitude capabilities of the day. AFSWC modified it to collect samples from nuclear mushroom clouds. Two tank-like fixtures with porous paper screens were mounted at the wing tips. All the pilots had to do was to fly through the clouds and pick up the invisible particles which were then sent to the laboratories for analysis where they calculated the efficiency of the bomb, i.e. the efficiency of the atom-splitting fission process before the big "BANG."

At one point I headed a project designed fire a rocket mounted on the B-57 through the nuclear clouds. Its purpose, to collect the samples and to radio the results back to base, obviating the need to expose air crews to radiation.

Also, during that assignment I was the guest of the Atomic Energy Commission in visiting a hush-hush plant in Kansas that fabricated nuclear weapons.

The Weapons Center commander was a Major General, now deceased. I would characterize him as an eccentric scientist. He held no staff meetings. He fired the Chief of Staff at 5 PM on a Christmas eve and later, fired me—without a word. I was never told why. The first thing I knew I was headed to Eniwetok, the last of the Pacific tests, without an assignment (some would say to Siberia). I made the most of it. As I hadn't yet checked out to pilot the B-57 I did check out as the rear seat operator of the switches that controlled the wingtip sample collectors. It was twice through the boiling clouds within minutes of detonation; it was quick in and out, as radiation accumulates with length of exposure. We wore dosimeters to check our exposure to radiation, which, for me, was 3 rads. The squadron commander had received 26 rads over several test series, with no apparent effects. The airplanes were washed with soap after exposure. I still have a full head of hair.

Upon returning from Eniwetok to Albuquerque I was made Deputy Commander of the Test Group, then later Commanding Officer. We spent our time putting together a tome for those who might be involved in further tests.

Years later and out of uniform in Asheville, North Carolina to give a talk, the host introduced me by making reference to flying through the nuclear clouds. He asked someone in the back of the room to turn out the lights, then said, "I want to see if he glows." I didn't.

6

STUTTER-STEPPING

The next phase of my life involved a bit of stutter-stepping. It was orders to a Troop Carrier Wing in Japan in 1958. Oops! No, the assignment folks meant the Air Force Pacific Communications Command, based at Wheeler Field, Oahu, Hawaii, where, scratching my head, I reported in. My new label: Director of Plans and Programs. Oh well, something new—totally new. All I knew about communications was how to talk on a telephone and turn on a TV set. To keep it short, after a few months of learning about high frequency, long distance transmitters and a field of antennas requiring large amounts of electric power (now outmoded) and taking a trip with the commander, Brigadier General Bernie Wooten, to Australia to open a new terminal there I asked him if I could transfer across the island to Headquarters, Pacific Air Forces (CINCPACAF) on Hickam Air Force Base. I had heard there was a vacancy for a deputy in Plans. He wasn't losing a valuable asset, which is probably why he said, "Yes," immediately. It was an amicable parting.

It was almost like returning home. I was now involved in applying, developing and perfecting the war plans I had worked on in the Pentagon. PACAF's role was to be prepared to act in any planned or emergency situation when so ordered and, also, to work with friendly forces, such as coordinating the provision of training cadres to South Vietnam. Yes, this was the phase of Vietnam where the South Vietnamese were going it alone against the Viet Cong. The Air Force negotiated for rights at air bases in Thailand, to be in position for possible future operations.

My boss, Dick Yudkin, a Colonel also, had an IQ about as high as anyone I've met. He could write a paper while conversing on the phone. It took me a while to catch on, but one of his techniques when he had a guest in his office, was to pop up from his desk, to start moving to the center of the room. The unknowing guest automatically stood and while still concentrating on the conversation was maneuvered to the door. Dick would say something like, "Thank you for coming," and close the door behind him.

After a personally satisfying tour in Hawaii it was back to the Pentagon.

7

The Vietnam War

It was the in the quiet fall of 1963 that I reported in the Pentagon for tour number two. This time to the Joint Staff, the staff supporting the Joint Chiefs of Staff (JCS) (at that time the corporate body served as advisors to the Secretary of Defense and the President; now the Chairman is the advisor to the President). Army General Earl Wheeler was Chairman; Air Force Lieutenant General David Burchinal, the Director of the Joint Staff; Rear Admiral Lloyd Mustin was Director of Operations; and Army Colonel Charley Mount, head of the Pacific Division, was my immediate boss.

Soon the quiet was shattered. The North Vietnamese gunboats attacked a US Navy ship in the Tonkin Gulf. This controversial event (contoversial in that there were questions as to whether it actually happened) was the trigger for the war. I'll skip to the day when the JCS were to vote as to whether to recommend to the Secretary of Defense, Robert McNamara, and the President that the US intervene on a massive scale. Having observed for several years the prelude of this action, I was thoroughly convinced that sending masses of troops to that area would be counterproductive. The superior firepower of US forces would be disadvantaged in jungle terrain, and our forces would bog down in such inhospitable surroundings. (Note the difference in terrain between the jungles of Vietnam and the Iraqi desert of Desert Storm and the difference in US casualties: 50,000 plus to 174). There were virtually no targets in North Vietnam of a strategic nature. I broke ranks when I walked out of the JCS "Purple Suit" area to the Air Force "Blue Suit" area to talk to an acquaintance whom I knew had the ear of the Air Force Chief, urging that the Chief vote "no." The JCS voted and the rest is history. Guess who wrote the message that started the deployment of more that 500,000 troops? Me. Had I been a service Chief I would have argued for all-out stand-off attacks against North Vietnam by air and naval forces.

Strategically, the Soviet Union used canny logic. They supplied North Vietnam with all the arms and equipment needed, including airplanes, radars and sophisticated surface to air missiles—and for the duration of the conflict Soviet supply ships were off limits to our air attacks. They also raised fears that China would intervene. The tally after it was all over: 50,000 plus Americans killed, South Vietnamese killed, wounded and displaced, in the millions and virtually zero for the Soviet Union. Our costs of supplying South Vietnam and transporting our more than 500,000 troops was considerably more than the Soviet's bill. In retrospect, had we not sent troops to Vietnam the outcome would have been but little different. The Soviet Communist system would have collapsed anyhow and Vietnam would be in its present independent state, tending towards a market economy, and we now do business with both.

I feel for the Vietnam veterans. Any one in the chain of command who had experience in combat was dedicated to providing the best in arms and supplies—and the all-important authority to fight the war to win. To me the textbook war was the Six Day War. Hit hard, achieve the objective! But in this case, political restrictions were applied which resulted in 12 bands being drawn across North Vietnam, and authority from the White House was needed to attack targets in the next band to the north. (We at CINCPAC, where I was next assigned, wrote a report at the end of the war on the negative impacts of the incrementalism involved). The Air War had been dubbed "Rolling Thunder," but political restrictions reduced it to a "Spasmodic Whimper." Needless to say, we spent a great deal of our time trying to get authority to use airpower to its potential. Again, an analogy with Desert Storm: there, air power targeted and hit everything but the population.

After two years in that Joint Staff office I was made Chief of the Pacific Division for my last year there. As the war developed it became my job to provide briefings for the JCS in the Command Center, usually about three times a week, on the progress (or lack thereof) of the war. At one point I briefed the Secretary of Defense, Robert McNamara and the JCS in the "tank" (the place where the

JCS held their meetings). The subject: tactical air warfare. Mr. Mc-Namara had questions about the need to reattack targets, especially bridges. With the aid of a map and photographs I explained the importance of North Vietnam's supply routes, particularly the many bridges and the rapidity with which they rebuilt them, at which they were experts. He seemed satisfied.

My new assignment was to CINCPAC, seconded to the Director of Operations, a Marine Major General, responsible for prosecuting the war and operating US forces in the Pacific Ocean area from Hawaii. The war progressed much the same, but gradually and spasmodically the restrictions on air operations were relaxed. We certainly put a great deal of effort into novel ways to hurt the enemy: devising ways to intercept enemy communications; and spoof the enemy with our communications; gaining authority to use new magnetic mines in waterways, remaining clear of Soviet ships; and expediting new techniques to defeat enemy radars and others. I toured the battlefields in South Vietnam, getting violently sick after eating a meal prepared by Vietnamese troops in the field. One site, miles from anywhere, was formerly occupied by American troops, and consisted of foxholes (they were more like rat holes) about two feet deep, with no cover, and had mines surrounding the area, which were later deactivated.This was home-in-the-field, no protection from the weather—or the enemy. I felt compassion for the ground forces that lived and fought under those conditions.

Back at CINCPAC, Richard Nixon, then a presidential candidate, stopped by on returning from a visit to Vietnam. Admiral Sharp and about five others, of which I was one, responded to his questions—and, of course, he was briefed on the need for more authority. Based on his questions I gained the impression that he was more interested in how the war was playing politically, rather than in helping the situation. Later, Vice President Humphrey stopped by. I briefed him on the latest air strikes and among others, one against a large steel mill near Hanoi.

Along the way I was invited to give a talk to the National War College in Taiwan on the subject, "US Warfare and Policy in Vietnam and the Pacific Area," which was tagged by the head of our US Advisory Group in Taiwan as, "one of the best and most effective contributions that we can make to further enhance relationships and the bonds of friendship. . . . " To my utter amazement, I was told later that my talk was made into a booklet and made available on the streets of Taipei—"utterly" because some of the material came from rather sensitive sources.

And then came the day when Admiral Sharp pinned on that first star. It was Brigadier General Kidd, who just maybe was the first Air Force officer be promoted to the rank of general while on joint duty.

8

Pentagon Tour Number Three

This time it was a distinct change. An assignment as Director, Personnel Planning and Programming in the Air Staff. After all, with 26 years in the Air Force, one is expected to be able to "climb every mountain." Most every assignment had been in operations or plans involving the combat forces, the really exciting jobs. But now, personnel? Hm! But lo and behold, it was fascinating. Besides, I now warranted an office of my own in the Pentagon—an outside room with a view of the Potomac River.

As was the custom, when an Air Force general officer checked into the Air Staff for duty in the Pentagon he made a courtesy call on the Air Force Chief. This was, in fact, a reunion, as four star Jack (John D.) Ryan was my first boss as a commissioned officer. He was a First Lieutenant, a section Chief in Hangar 4, Kelly Field, Texas. I graduated from Advanced Flying School and was commissioned a Second Lieutenant on October 4, 1940. The next day I received my rating as a pilot and was immediately made an instructor of five students (imagine a college student becoming a professor upon graduating); I was one of five instructors assigned to Jack Ryan. (In all I graduated 40 students). I had talked to Jack only once in the intervening years—in 1942 at Lubbock, Texas where he was a Captain in the Bombardier School. I found him atop an eight foot high motorized rig, peering into a bombsight, homing in on a target on the floor. This was his project and gave student bombardiers a feel for the real thing. The only thing missing was the roar of the engines.

In his Pentagon office we had a fine time reminiscing. As I was walking to the door he said "Oh, by the way, Jack, the Air Force doesn't have a personnel plan." I turned, nodded, and said "Yes, sir" and departed. Eight months later there was a Personnel Plan, eight volumes of it, approved by General Ryan and the Secretary of the Air Force, and endorsed by the Department of Defense. It was in this period that my second star was pinned on me.

Within my directorate a planning office was set up, headed by Colonel Charles Robb; he was provided with twelve high-powered young officers, some of whom were whiz kids on the computer, even in 1968. The plan served many functions.

In the US Air Force Personnel Plan, much like engineers design airplanes to have unique characteristics, such as for bombing, transporting or fighting, we designed the entire Air Force military personnel force.

The original officer force looked like a pyramid with its top sliced off, the vertical dimension was the thirty-year mark, by which time only a very few officers were retained. During wars officers were called back to active duty and, of course, officers in the service remained, and a larger number than normal were recruited. This created bulges on the side slopes of the pyramid which caused problems. The enlisted profile was similar.

In just this one example, the benefits of macro-planning can be appreciated. As a bulge was created, pilot training required as many as ten air bases equipped with training aircraft, instructors and support personnel. In the ensuing valley, between wars, pilot training required only one equipped air base to satisfy the requirement. By smoothing the bulges and valleys enormous savings were accrued. Today, training a single pilot exceeds $1 million.

Similar significant savings were made through a new retraining system for both officers and enlisted personnel. As another example, far more enlisted air police men and women are needed in their early years; through retraining they fill other required skills.

The task involved flowing personnel through the system to meet and fulfill skill requirements. As I recall, there were about 900 enlisted skills and 400 officer skills in the Air Force.

Promotions of both officers and enlisted personnel were either fast or slow, depending on whether one was on a bulge or in a valley. Again, smoothing the bulges and valleys alleviates that problem, a key factor in retention of personnel.

This summary of the plan is but a tip-of-the-iceberg , which initially included eight volumes, about six inches high—stacked one on the other.

Together with the plan, a management system was set up to get on top of the hundreds of requirements involving Air Force personnel: by the Air Force; the Department of Defense; and the Congress. Anyone could quite readily find the designated, informed officer on any issue involving personnel.

Speaking of the big bucks, among other responsibilities I was the officer accountable for $7 billion, or almost a third of the Air Force budget, the largest of the three services. It was at the time when Secretary of the Air Force, Seamans tagged the Air Force as "the largest business in the world." Interestingly, several years earlier, while preparing to return to the mainland from Hawaii for a new assignment, I had requested to be sent to the Harvard Business School (my brother was a graduate). The personnel people responded, telling me that the Air Force would not pay for the transportation back to the mainland. Of course, I offered to pay. The answer again, no! The irony of it all! Oh well, Econ 101, Money and Banking and very few other business courses in college got me by—together with overtime, some common sense, imagination and a lot of good help.

Another of the actions taken gave me a special feeling of accomplishment. One day Colonel Jeanne Holm, head of Women in the Air Force (WAF), made an appointment. To make the story short, by the end of the meeting Jeanne and I had agreed on a policy that "all women in the Air Force could enter any career field and any job for which they were physiologically able." As I recall it opened up twenty-six career fields to women, save those which were prohibited by law which, at that time, included combat and pilot training, for example. Jeanne went on to a job in the White House, retiring as a Major General.

I could go on and on. There were other fascinating jobs in the personnel planning function. About ten boards and committees came with the assignment: individual training requirements; allocating the profits of the Army-Air Force Exchanges to build recreational facilities, etc., etc.

One day my boss called me in and said, "As of now you are the Air Force Drug Abuse Officer." It was just about as brief as that. I'd never known anyone who used drugs. It was off quickly to an Air Force facility in Denver where a handful of enlisted personnel were being treated and counseled. I spoke to several of them, talking about their problems and experiences. The reporting system and the Air Force-wide treatment of cases was soon set up. Later, it was off to Congress several times to testify as to Air Force programs and progress, travel costs and other issues. On one occasion a congressman blistered me for the fact that men were using drugs while on duty in an air defense unit. Not having heard of it I told him I would check into it and respond. I called to tell him that it involved another service and referred him to the proper authority. Thankfully, in the Air Force the problem was minimal, but even one person on drugs in our precision and potentially dangerous activities was one too many.

9

Beautiful Rome

In 1992 my final assignment was as the Chief, Military Assistance Advisory Group, Italy, with offices and staff across the street (Via Venato) from the US Embassy. My mission in a broad sense was to handle military matters, including weapons procurement, between the two governments. The chain of command was unique. I reported to Ambassador Graham Martin and attended his staff meetings, and reported to US CINCEUR in Germany and, also, dealt directly with the office of the Secretary of Defense in Washington.

Along with the representational quarters—a penthouse apartment (paid for by the embassy), there were two US Air Force aides, a chauffeur and an Italian Air Force Lieutenant for an aide.

Thankfully the international scene was relatively tranquil, although the Communists were trying their best to take over Italy— and did elect a Communist as Mayor of Bologna.

In sum, I looked after ongoing programs, started some new ones, called on every Italian service chief and many major field commanders around the country, all of whom I must say, were most gracious.

And then, I retired, in 1974.

As a sort of postscript to my 31 years in uniform I thought this bit of information would be of interest to young people in the military services. Recently I asked the Air Force Personnel Center at Randolph Air Force Base in Texas for information (which was provided expeditiously by Sergeant Stephen Heitkamp).

Here was this kid (me) who left college in the middle of his junior year to join the Army Air Corps to learn how to fly. I retired as a two star general, a major general. The data from the Sergeant indicated that I was 54th from the top of 196 generals in the Air Force at my retirement date (I say 54 for my ego's sake, which put the other 142 other generals behind me). And this in a force with 110,419 officers, in a total force of 639,482.

The message I want to send is that, regardless of your degrees (in the '50s a baccalaureate degree was required to become an officer), your race or whatever, that by applying yourself you can reach the top—or close to it. To me the single most important factor is one's application. In other words, whatever assignment or job you are given, take full responsibility for doing it to the best of your ability no matter what. In the military your country depends on it. One of the officers I worked with in the Pentagon had a favorite expression, "That's good enough for government work." I cringed when I heard it. There are no excuses.

The promotion system in the services is about as good as can be devised, so failure to advance is not an excuse either.

And I add to you young people, civilian or in uniform, don't get the idea from this book that I'm out to decimate military forces. Far from it. We will need a strong, able, responsive military force as far into the future as I can see.

In case you are wondering what those awards and decorations were in that photo at Chapter 1, they are: two Distinguished Service Medals, Silver Star, two Distinguished Flying Crosses, three Air Medals, two Legion of Merit, Air Force Commendation Medal, the Croix de Guerre avec Palme, the Berlin Airlift Award and other awards. Rated a Command Pilot, I flew 7,500 hours including airline time (or 10 1/2 months in the air).

10

Retirement?

After 31 years of active duty I retired on January 1, 1974. So, after all the courtesy calls on Italian officials and the Ambassador, it was depart Rome, cross the United States, visit friends and relatives, and depart the West Coast for Australia. Why to Australia? In retrospect, a lark more than anything.

Aussies aren't keen on hiring foreigners, but after a few months of looking I landed a job with Leyland Australia (Ford and General Motors had plants far removed from Sydney) which made the only car designed in Australia, the P-76, a four-door sedan, and the Moke, a Jeep-like vehicle, as well as buses and trucks. I guess it was because the Aussie CEO was a Harvard Business School grad that he hired a Yank. During the interview I think my clincher comment was, "I've always tried to leave a job in better condition than when I started." But as I soon learned, their systems were so poor that 3000 newly built cars were sitting on the lot awaiting one or more parts. I was assigned to the logistic/supply side (which I successfully avoided in the military) as assistant to the #1 logistician. In two months the lot was cleared. But about a year later a young Britisher from Leyland UK headquarters arrived, whose assignment we soon learned was to shut down the passenger car lines. There went the job.

It was back to the good old US to look for a place to live. How about Pebble Beach? Why not? With a bit of profit from the sale of the Sydney condominium, a modest house in Pebble Beach was within reach. Incidentally, I, a Yank, was elected by my fellow Aussie condo owners in Cremorne, a suburb of Sydney, to be the President of the condo Owners' Association. The building was twelve stories high, of novel construction, built of concrete slab walls, floors and

ceilings. Inside, one couldn't tell the difference from a convention-
ally built structure. One would think that this type of construction
would feel cold, but not so in the moderate temperature in Sydney.
It has never snowed there. The view was spectacular, overlooking
Broken Bay. I could look down on my small sailboat—which Aussies
called "yachts." It was a 26–footer, slept four and had a galley. There
were harrowing experiences, like being caught in a "Southerly
Buster," at sea about twenty miles north of Sydney Harbor—sails
ripped, motor zonked, no lifelines bordering the deck. Fortunately a
power boat came along and threw a line for a tow to a safe haven.

Then it was off to Pebble Beach, to try my hand in real estate,
for a time working for a realty company, until J. B. Kidd and Associates was incorporated. Why not make a few bucks? "Few" is the
correct word—as later I made more selling the house than I did in
brokering real estate, a windfall from the exorbitant interest rates of
the day. Among a lot of other activities, I served as head of the local
citizens group, supporting the new Monterey Institute of International Studies. There were some fine parties at interesting homes in
the Carmel-Pebble Beach area.

It was during those Pebble Beach days in the early '80s that I
woke up. The arms race between the US and the Soviets had been
under way for well over thirty years. I got to thinking about the lose-
lose situation we were in. The pall of instant annihilation hung over,
not only our heads, but the Soviets, too—as well as the rest of the
world. There were a few signs of sanity: the SALT (Strategic Arms
Limitation Treaty) of 1972, which put a temporary lid on intercontinental ballistic missiles, thus halting a segment of the arms race. The
Anti-Ballistic Missile (ABM) Treaties of 1972 and 1974 placed strin-
gent limits on missile defenses. SALT ll , of 1979, set limits of 2400
on missile launchers and heavy bombers on each side, although President Carter withdrew his support after the Soviets invaded Afghanistan. At this stage, both sides were straining economically, the end of
the arms race was nowhere in sight, and relations between the two
sides were frigid. No arms reduction treaties were in hand. Each side
continued to try to out-build the other, locked in a deadly embrace,
unable to disengage. Our national debt trebled in a few short years in
that period to $5.5 trillion, assisted by the Strategic Defense Initiative,
the US shield against enemy missiles. Now nineteen years later, the national debt is still at an astronomical level, about $3.7 trillion.

I began speaking out locally—at the Rotary and Kiwanis Clubs in Monterey and Carmel, at the Monterey Institute of International Studies and the County Democratic Committee. When I arrived to give a talk at the Republican Committee, the Chairman announced to me and the assemblage that they didn't want to hear me; hearing about ending the arms race with the Soviets must have been too much to stomach. Ironically, it was a Republican president—President Reagan—who later reined in the arms race.

Those were macho days. I had joined the ranks of the many organizations which were speaking out about the tenuous situation, and what I called , the lose-lose situation.

It must have been the planner in me because one day I went into my study and began developing "The Strategic Cooperation Initiative (SCI) or the 'Star Light' Strategy," a takeoff on President Reagan's Strategic Defense Initiative (SDI). "SCI-Starlight" developed into a six part plan to end the arms race and the Cold War, so constructed that the US and the Soviets could simply say "yes," thus approving the plan in principle. People gathered around. Help was in abundance. A non-profit organization, tagged "Bridges World Wide," was formed. The speaking engagement invitations came more often. The Cold War hung over the land like an icy, wet blanket. The American people were concerned. Altogether I made some seventy or eighty talks in thirteen states from California to Maine, and even in Moscow—on three occasions. Audience reaction? All the way from hero to traitor.

I attended a conference held in Moscow in the mid-eighties entitled "New Thinking in the Nuclear Age: Social Inventions for the Third Millennium." Interestingly, that organization was funded by Soviet citizens, not by the government. About thirty Americans and forty Soviets met to discuss the issues freely, something truly remarkable during the ongoing frigid diplomatic relationship. I made a presentation, having passed out a SCI—Star Light flyer, translated into Russia. The head of the Russian contingent asked, "What do you want me to do?" I replied, "Sign it." He did.

In view of the frigidity of US—Soviet relations, I thought it wise to inform our State Department and the Soviet Embassy in Washington that I was going to the Soviet Union and why. I talked to the #2 man on the Soviet Desk at the State Department. Talking *at* him would be a more accurate description. He simply would not discuss "a way out of the arms race." The Soviet diplomat was more cordial. He escorted me to the front door of their Embassy in Washington where we said our good-byes. When I was about twenty feet down the walk he hailed me, approached and talked about my getting him speaking engagements in the US. Later it struck me that for reasons of his own, he wanted me on the film that our FBI was no doubt taking of my departure from the second story apartment across the street. On my return from the Soviet Union the FBI did invite me to their office in Monterey to question me about the trip. I heard nothing more about it. Thank God for freedom of speech in this nation.

While in Moscow on that trip I visited the United States-Canada Institute, a Soviet think-tank headed by Georgi Arbatov. I asked what his views were as to a meeting between retired Soviet and US generals and admirals. He nodded his head. It was there I met retired Lieutenant General Mikhail Milshtein. We would meet again.

In April, 1987 a meeting between American and Russian retired "flag officers" did occur, organized by the Center for Defense Information, a Washington think-tank with which I was affiliated. A rather signal event, considering the tense diplomatic climate! Recall that the Soviet Union was tagged with appellations such as "the evil empire," and "you can't trust the Russians." We were concerned that the State Department wouldn't allow the Russians' entry into the US. The Soviets did arrive. Secretary of Defense Weinberger declined the invitation to send an observer. Incidentally, all the Russians spoke English. Of course, none of us spoke Russian.

I thought the discussions were groundbreaking and of considerable significance, so at my suggestion the apparent meeting of the minds was put on paper. Here is the report as recorded in my 1988 book:

Epilogue

What About a Nuclear Free World?

What Soviet Generals and Admiral Say

A meeting of historic importance took place on April 21–22, 1987. It was the first meeting between retired Soviet and American Generals and Admirals. Eight Soviets and seven Americans met in Washington, D.C. sponsored by the Center for Defense Information (CDI), though one of the Soviet Generals was on active duty with their Defense Ministry. CDI's Director, Admiral La Rocque, informed the group that Mr. Weinberger, Secretary of Defense, had been invited to send a representative but had declined. The group of fifteen represented about 500 years of active military service. All the Americans and the Soviets had participated in World War ll, while the Americans had participated in as many as three wars.

During the two day conference, differences of opinion were expressed, but soon paled in contrast to the scope and import of the specific agreements reached. Adding to the remarkable agreements, was the way it came about. The flag officers found it impossible to stay within the original agenda, which was designed to evoke safety measures pertaining to opposing forces in Europe. In the free exchange of ideas and opinions we moved inevitably to the far more basic issues. And, it was remarkable that in spite of the fact that no consensus was required, just thirty minutes before the end of the conference, agreements were reached and a communiqué settled.

The conference received sparse attention by the media. It deserved far wider dissemination.

It was rewarding to have been a participant in the conference. Savor the following record of the meeting:

Agreed Statement of Retired Soviet and American Generals and Admirals
(Drafted by Rear Admiral Eugene Carroll, US Navy)

Recognizing that continuing arms buildup in the United States and the Soviet Union is increasing the risk of nuclear war and reducing the security of both nations; agreeing that a positive program of cooperative actions is necessary to reverse the arms buildup; and, concerned that discussions concerning arms reductions so far have not produced significant improvements, it is fully agreed that the following actions are not only urgently needed to improve the relationship between our nations and to create the confidence necessary for future cooperative measures, but such actions would also serve the security interests of all nations.

1. Nuclear weapons cannot be used for any rational military or political purpose. Actions to reduce nuclear weapons substantially

must be accelerated with the objective of eliminating them entirely. As first step, intermediate range missiles in Europe should be eliminated immediately.

2. All nuclear testing and tests of new nuclear delivery systems must cease.

3. No weapons should be designed, tested or deployed for use in space including weapons for the destruction of satellites and ballistic missiles.

4. Existing arms control agreements including the ABM treaty should continue to be strictly observed.

5. Major reductions should be made in conventional forces, and all troops should be removed from foreign countries.

6. The US and the USSR should take the lead in reducing the sale of arms to developing nations to prevent the proliferation of nuclear weapons in the world.

7. The US and the USSR should intensify their cooperation and enlist the support from all nations to prevent the proliferation of nuclear weapons in the world.

These broad understandings and specific agreements readily reached by retired generals and admirals of the United States and the Soviet Union suggest the value of similar meetings of active-duty military professionals from both sides. Such meetings by serving officers could lead to better mutual understanding and formulation of practical actions for agreement and implementation by our national leaders."

<table>
<tr><td>Michail A. Milshtein,
Lieutenant General
Soviet Army (Ret.)</td><td>Gene R. La Rocque,
Rear Admiral
US Navy (Ret.)</td></tr>
</table>

Commentary on the above. This is getting ahead of the story, but there has been significant action in the reduction of nuclear weapons with much, much more to do; reduction of conventional forces has been considerable and, as to the proliferation of nuclear weapon actions, not much has been accomplished. To the contrary, several more nations have joined the club. But on all the other items—more than a decade later—there is intense current effort devoted to getting ready for fighting in the next battle zone, space. And as opposed to taking preventive action many in Congress want to scrap the Anti-Ballistic Missile (ABM) Treaty; selling arms is a mega-business; and the US now has the most powerful military force by far. And then there is the expansion of NATO to the east, which could slow or halt heretofore cooperative measures with Russia, including the reduction of nuclear weapons and alienating the Russians.

There was another trip to Russia. The Russian generals and admirals invited us for meetings in Moscow and Leningrad (now St. Petersburg). The spirit of unanimity continued, even in a public forum in the latter city. The meetings received virtually no press in the US but considerable in the USSR.

On one of these visits I furnished the Russian generals and admirals with copies of my 1988 "Strategic Cooperation Initiative-Star Light" book. The one general of the group who was not retired, but an active duty member of the Russian General staff, later told me that he had given his copy to the chief of the Russian military staff who, in turn, had given it to President Gorbachev. I would like to think that SCI-Starlight played a role in ending the Cold War. And I note that now the two nations are cooperating in space ventures and actually reducing nuclear weapons.

Each presidential candidate of the day and their wives received two copies of my book; each member of the Congress also received two copies.

It was nine years later, in 1997, that other retired officers followed suit, spearheaded by Retired General Lee Butler, the former Strategic Air Command commander. About 100 retired generals and admirals (including those of us at the 1987 Washington meeting), from many nations joined the chorus for the elimination of nuclear weapons, including three American four-star generals.

Now, in a completely different vein, I quote a passage from my 1988 book, The Strategic Cooperation Initiative or the 'Star Light' Strategy, which affected me deeply then—and still does.

Impacts on Society

Just recently, work by some specialists has gotten under way to understand the impact on a society living under the threat of nuclear annihilation. One such effort is that of the Center for Psychological Studies in the Nuclear Age in Cambridge. At this point more is known about effects on children than on adults. Certainly the 'now' syndrome in our youth as well as adults is abetted if not caused by this pall. Dr. Robert Jay Lifton testified before a House committee that "There is increasing evidence that young people doubt that they can live out their full lives. . . . No single behavior pattern of symptoms can be said to be caused entirely by this imagery of extinction—young people still go through ordinary struggles around family,work and play, achievement and self-worth—but neither is anything in their lives entirely free of this disturbing image." He went on to say that "Young people, like others in our society, come to lead a double life. On the one hand they go about their every day activities . . . for their preparation for adult life. But on the other hand, they express the fearful sense that there will be no adult existence. Then, amidst all this talk of national security, we experience a considerable threat to family security."

I'm waiting for research to confirm my gut feeling that to a large extent alcoholism, drug use with its associated crime, and teen pregnancy are by-products of the nuclear arms race; more recently we find that teen suicides have trebled in the past twenty years. These effects, I believe, can be measured in monumental misery as well as billions and billions of dollars of costs to society, business and government each year. Today, we pay a tremendous social toll preparing for war, a war that can never be fought. We should know more about this toll and its costs. Again, Congress would do well to subsidize these investigations.

I've highlighted the above because even today we focus almost exclusively on the hardware involved in our conundrum, paying no attention to the human being, particularly our children. I have the strong feeling that our monumental crime rates today are but a continuation of the those fostered during the Cold War, that the impact on those who grew up under that pall of annihilation have been passed along through several generations down to the present.

I harken back to the innocence of college days just before WW ll at Oberlin College in Ohio. A classmate of mine was thrown out of college for drinking one glass of whiskey; it was common knowledge on campus that a freshman girl of 18 didn't know how babies were born; the word "drugs" was unknown—there were none.

Contrast this to today. The effects discussed above have permutated and mutated through five wars this century, through several generations. As I am writing this, six boys, ages 11 to 14, are in a juvenile detention center awaiting trial in my home town, Charlottesville, Virginia—for gang-raping an 11 year old girl—in her own home. The 14 year-old may be tried as an adult and could be incarcerated for life, the others, to age twenty-one. On last night's news an MIT freshman, a handsome fellow, died from binge-drinking whiskey—his blood alcohol five times the legal limit for driving a car. We house nearly two million prisoners in our jails, about one in every 135 Americans. You know all the rest. There seems to be a direct correlation between the state of world insecurity and national, community and a personal sense of insecurity. A clear example is that of the hippie movement during the Vietnam War. Millions changed their very life style. I note that the massacre at Columbine High School—with many to follow quickly—took place during the Kosovo violence. When the world is in turmoil, it seems to translate down through to the individual. A study of that correlation should not be all that difficult and I think, would be an extremely worthwhile project.

My 1988 book ended with this paragraph:

Prepared to Meet the Challenge?

We are now facing the most serious issues ever encountered by human beings. We don't have much time. If we succeed in reversing these man-made problems, all of which affect everyone on this planet, we will indeed find an existence far closer to Utopia. We know the alternative. The great question before us is whether we have the foresight and fortitude to solve them. Or will fear, profit, power, ego, political or other divisiveness cause us to fail? It will be the greatest test of our democratic process. We will get what we deserve.

The Cold War is over, but now, a decade later, we are still confronted with monumental problems. The possibility of annihilation, seemingly remote, still remains. It will be many years before nuclear weapons can be eliminated, yes, it is still a distant dream.

New weapons of mass destruction are in many hands. Even more powerful weapons are on the drawing board. New theaters for new types of warfare have opened.

The solution to these problems have eluded us. Preventive measures have been virtually non-existent. As progress is made, other serious threats arise. It's like walking up a down-escalator, unable to move ahead.

New approaches are vital if solutions are to be found. Part II offers solutions to "Meet the Challenge," ending with A New Strategy for America.

Part II

A New Strategy for America

In Part II an assessment is made of America's politico-military experience in the world during this century—the bloodiest century ever—and, based on the many changes that have occurred, the result, a national course of action for the 21st Century. Indeed: A New Strategy for America. Because of the many elements involved, as you read on it may seem that they are separate and unrelated. Please be assured that they are all connected and will coalesce at the end. I see it as the placing of tiles of different colors, shapes and sizes on a wall with the end result a pleasing mosaic, one even of sublimity.

11

It Was Ever Thus

As in the *Homo erectus* Age, *Homo sapiens* found different and more efficient ways to maim and kill their own, starting with the stone, then the club, the bow and arrow, the gun, the tank, poison gas, biological weapons, and the A-bomb. Now in the *Homo destructus* Age, a single thermonuclear weapon is capable of causing major cities to disappear. Reflect for a moment on the effects of just Washington, DC and New York City disappearing: utter, utter devastation, and chaos throughout the nation. With the detonation of thousands of such weapons, visualize civilization simply disappearing—at best leaving pockets of mutilated, disfigured, poisoned, starving survivors in the global fallout. If we let this happen we will fail our Creator miserably, having so misused His gift of free will.

Is this notion of destruction exaggerated? No. Can it happen? Yes, by a national leader uttering one word or simply pushing a button—conceivably acting on fragmentary or even faulty information. Even more bizarre, picture a psychotic aide to a national leader pressing the "doomsday" button, leaving the earth devoid of human and animal life—or imagine a nuclear blast caused by an electrical failure or a short circuit in missile tracking radars! What words are there to describe the situation in which we have placed ourselves? Idiocy? Absurdity? Insanity? None seem wholly adequate.

I am keenly aware and supermotivated as to these consequences because of my intimate familiarity with nukes. As Deputy Chief of Staff, Operations of the Air Force Special (Nuclear) Weapons Center, for scientific purposes—within minutes of detonation—I flew through nuclear clouds voluntarily, during the Pacific tests at Eniwetok.

And now, even deadlier weapons are on the drawing board, weapons that will trivialize even the thermonuclear weapon in destructive power.

If a species of animals had such a penchant for killing its own it would be studied carefully to determine the source of such sadism. In the case of mankind it appears that fear, selfishness, envy, retribution, covetousness, greed, as well as individual and national egoism, has been the driving force—a powerful force in the *Homo erectus* Age—a force which now, in the present *Homo destructus* Age, has the potential of evermore massive destruction due to the misuse of technological advances. We still carry that eon-old baggage. Changing our ways after millions of years will not be easy but it is crucial that we do so, or be doomed—possibly by one person.

The challenge: bring into being Worldwide Rule of Law—which is derived in the main from age-old moral and religious principles—with an effective enforcement capability, to find ways to prevent arms races, wars and violence in order to live in harmony on our planet, which grows ever smaller.

12

What Got Me Really Worked Up

Our nation was heavily involved in five major wars this century, from first to last, one beginning on average every sixteen years. Shocking, isn't it? The United States instigated none of them. In one, our territory—Pearl Harbor—was attacked. In the other four, World War I, Korea, Vietnam and the Gulf War, our nation came to the aid of friendly nations.

The toll of Americans in uniform killed this century: 620,000, with 1,131, 000 wounded.[1] Worldwide, war related deaths total 110,000,000, mostly civilians. There have been 250 wars, making the 20th Century the bloodiest ever, six times bloodier than the 19th Century.[2]

What I'm worked up about is the fact that far too little is being done to prevent a repetition of this century in the next. One would have thought that at the end of the Cold War with its US-Soviet arms race the stops would have been pulled, and that a major, integrated, overarching prevention effort by the United States, leader of the Free World, would have been made. It has not happened. Instead, like lemmings, we continue to concentrate on preparing for the next war.

I had expected that the candidates in the 1996 presidential campaign would have raised these issues, would have some new solutions, would offer plans. Instead, there was a stony silence on what

[1]The World Almanac and Book of Facts, 1999. Copyright 1999. PRIMEDIA Reference Inc., One International Boulevard, Suite 630, Mahway, NJ 07495

[2]Reproduced, with permission, from "World Military and Social Expenditures"1996 by Ruth Leger Sivard, Copyright 1996 by World Priorities, Box 25140, Washington, DC, 20007, USA

I considered to be the most important issues of our times: war and peace, our national security—in an ever more dangerous world. The candidates and the government concentrated on domestic affairs: Medicare, Social Security, the deficit, fixing the budget, the president's problems. Yes, they all need attention, but their solutions would be far simpler if the monumental expenditures for preparation for war were reduced through a prevention agenda. Waging peace through prevention would be far more cost-effective than our current inaction.

Currently our debt is $3.7 trillion—due mainly to past wars—which is about 45 percent of the total Gross Domestic Product. It is the taxpayers who are still shelling out more than $200 billion in interest on the debt each year, chiefly because of past wars.

If we become embroiled in another major war—due in the year 2007 based on the experience of this century's wars—we would see our domestic programs again go askew. Recall that at the close of the Cold War our national debt reached $5.5 trillion.

13

The Story of Arms Races

Arms Control, Reduction and PREVENTION

The world's best known arms race began at the end of WW II.

Ruth Lager Sivard in *World Military and Social Expenditures* informs that "The world stockpile [of nuclear weapons] grew enormously, and by 1986 reached the equivalent of 18,000 megatons, (18,000,000,000,000 tons of high explosive power), that as much as $4,000,000,000 of America's public treasure may have been spent over the years (and perhaps another $4 trillion among the other four acknowledged nuclear powers). . . ."[1]

"Between 1950 and 1990, the United States spent an estimated $12 trillion on defense (valued in 1997 dollars). . . . The best [albeit much more uncertain] estimates are that the USSR and its dependencies may have spent an equivalent of nearly $12 trillion as well. . . ."[2] (For anyone wishing to pursue the study of the arms race and disarmament see the references at the end of the chapter.)

Fueled by the attack on Pearl Harbor the United States built the first A-bomb. The Soviets followed shortly thereafter, in 1949. Then the thermonuclear bomb, ditto the Soviets. Then the United States built the intercontinental ballistic missile (ICBM), ditto the Soviets.

---

[1]Reproduced, with permission, from"World Military and Social Expenditures"1996 by Ruth Leger Sivard, copyright (C) 1996 by World Priorities, Box 25140, Washington, DC, 20007 USA

[2]Options and Opportunities: Arms Control and Disarmament for the 21st century, by Jonathan Dean and Jeffrey Laurenti, Copyright 1997 by the United Nations Association of the United States of America, (UNA-USA), New York.

Then the United States introduced multiple warheads. Then the missile submarine. The Soviets followed. Then came the shorter range, theater missiles.

If we mark the end of WW ll as the beginning of the nuclear arms race, it took twenty-seven years for the two sides to come to their senses, to limit or reduce nuclear weapons, which by then could end civilization.

The first important agreement was the Limited Test Ban Treaty of 1963, signed by the US, the USSR and Great Britain, which prohibited testing nuclear weapons in space, above ground and under water. (I took part in the tests at Eniwetok in 1954).

It was not until nine years later, in 1972, that the US and the Soviets agreed to limit nuclear weapons, in SALT 1 (Strategic Arms Limitation Treaty) to a five-year freeze on testing and deployment of intercontinental ballistic missiles and submarine-launched missiles, as well as placing a ceiling on offensive nuclear weapons. As a result of the SALT 1 negotiations, the all-important ABM—the Anti-Ballistic Missile Treaty, was signed in 1972, which limited each side to two sites of 100 missile launchers. Two years later each agreed to reduce to one site each. The treaty is still in effect. The SALT 1 Treaty was extended in 1977. Had this not been agreed and without the ABM Treaty, each side could have continued an open-ended deployment of more missiles: more missiles, more defense, more defense, more missiles, ad infinitum.

SALT ll, agreed in 1979, placed a ceiling of 2400 missile launchers and heavy bombers, and 1320 ICBMs and submarine launched missiles on each side, but was never ratified by the Senate.

In 1983 President Reagan pushed the Strategic Defense Initiative (SDI), dubbed "Star Wars." More on this later.

Finally, in 1991, forty-six years after the start of the Arms Race, the first nuclear arms reduction treaty, START 1, was signed by presidents Bush and Gorbachev, in which they agreed to reduce strategic offensive nuclear weapons by one-third over seven years. Two years later Presidents Bush and Gorbachev agreed in START ll on another reduction, about one-third of the then-existing numbers of weapons over a period of ten years. It took four more years for the US to ratify it; the Russian DUMA has yet to ratify it. The enlargement of NATO to the east in 1999 could delay the DUMA's approval indefinitely. Should enlarging NATO to the east derail nuclear arms reductions it will have been a very bad deal, scuttling all-important nuclear reduction, the only threat to the very survival of the US—in echange for the extremely remote attack on NATO nations. Work on START lll is poised to begin only after START ll is ratified by the Russian DUMA. Until this happens we are left with the problem of how and when to get the nuclear reduction process restarted?

Thus far the US and Russia have reduced their 11,000 active strategic "nuclear warheads and bombs to below 9,000 countable warheads and 1,800 delivery vehicles . . . the *reduced* stockpile represents 727 times the 11 megatons of explosive power in this century's three major wars. . . ."[1]

START Il prescribes reductions to the 3,500 level of bombs and warheads, then down by one-third, to be reached in the year 2007. It would eliminate land based-multiple warhead missiles entirely. Three other nations, the UK, France and China, have from 200 to 800 each. They are yet to be parties to arms reduction efforts, as are the several "undeclared" nuclear powers with fewer weapons.

A number of ideas for the further drastic reductions of nuclear weapons to the low hundreds of weapons, or even elimination, are being discussed. Inexorably the other three nuclear nations will be brought into the negotiations. Experts' estimates cover a range up to twenty years before these low levels can be achieved.

As the number of weapons becomes smaller, each side reviews its national security position more carefully; maintaining a balance of the offense-defense mix of weapons becomes more critical. And needless to say, the parties involved must be mindful of political moves in order that plans and negotiations for further reductions will not be derailed. The fact that current negotiations are between democratic governments should facilitate mutual reductions.

The Chemical Weapons Treaty has been signed by 120 nations in 1993; the US ratified in 1997. Although more than 100 nations have agreed to prohibit development, testing and stockpiling of biological weapons, research has not ended.

Despite these agreements, in early 1998 Secretary of Defense Cohen cited the fact that at least twenty-five nations are at work on nuclear and chemical, as well as biological weapons.

A list of treaties is shown at the end of this chapter.

Getting to Zero

In 1997 more than 60 retired admirals and generals from many nations, including General Lee Butler, Air Force, former CINC SAC, General Andrew Goodpaster, US Army, SACEUR, and General Charles Horner, Air Force, Commander, Space Command—and, yes, I was one of them—went public and proposed the elimination of nuclear weapons, indicating that they are useless. I say more than useless. They are the only weapons that can eliminate life on this planet. As you have already noted, I had been making the case to zero nuclear weapons since the early 1980s. Then in 1987, there was that meeting in Washington with eight Soviet and seven retired generals and admirals who agreed that nuclear weapons should be destroyed. No military commander could assure the Commander in Chief that he could win a nuclear battle. Indeed, Presidents Reagan and Gorbachev agreed that "A nuclear war cannot be won and must never be fought."

Acquiring or having nuclear—or other weapons of mass destruction—merely challenges others to follow suit. Should another major arms race begin, nuclear or non-nuclear, our president may find himself again playing one-upmanship with megalomaniacs, the likes of Hitler, Tojo or Stalin which, with even more powerful weapons, could end civilization in the twinkling of an eye. In the Cuban Missile Crisis, where we came closest to an exchange of nuclear weapons, we can be thankful that Khruschev was levelheaded enough to back down.

Star Wars

I quote again from my 1988 book, *The Strategic Cooperation Initiative or the 'Star Light' Strategy:*

"President Reagan proposed the Strategic Defense Initiative (SDI) or Star Wars in 1983, a plan designed to make nuclear weapons 'impotent and obsolete' by installing a protective shield to destroy incoming missiles. His vision has great appeal, yet the growing debate over Star Wars has raised serious questions. Some reputable scientists and even statesmen claim, as do I, that it is un-workable and, moreover, presents a grave danger to the United States. Arguments against it include the ease of underflying, decoying, and countering; cost estimates run to $1 trillion. Most importantly, the deterrence from the existing parity of nuclear weapons will be lost. A very perilous imbalance will result.

Star Wars would have inherent offensive, as well as defensive capabilities. It is not necessarily non-nuclear as we have been told. Star Wars envisages only continued reliance on military hardware, and would mean breaking the vital ABM Treaty."

Military hardware will never solve our differences with the Soviet Union.

The estimated cost of the original Star Wars 1983 five-year program was $26 billion, with Congress voting $3-5 billion a year. The ostensible purpose: to research basic physical and scientific principles. The US reportedly spent upwards of $50 billion—some report $90 billion on Star Wars—with no useable hardware to show since its inception—and we are now again spending each year on the new Star Wars. Its origin resulted from one-upmanship between the conservatives and liberals in the Congress. The Joint Chiefs of Staff went along for the ride.

I recall watching Secretary of Defense Weinberger on TV in the mid-'80s testifying before the Congress to the effect that Star Wars would be 99% effective. My instant thought was—which 100 American cities will be destroyed with the remaining 1%? Note: As no hardware was in hand, no testing was possible, no success rates could have been determined.

I've long had the notion that Star Wars was designed by the US to make the stakes in the arms race appear so high that the USSR might throw in the towel, simply to find a way out of the burdensome arms race by some means. The $50 billions or so, should have produced some sort of workable missile defense hardware, but it didn't. Certainly Secretary of Defense Weinberger's "99 %" claim was totally implausible—and groundless; the WW II Luftwaffe's air defense was only about 6% effective—but having been on the receiving end, it was quite daunting at that. In my book, a 99% effective system against nuclear weapons isn't feasible.

Star Wars II

In recent debates many members of Congress have pressed for a missile defense, arguing that the US is vulnerable to an attack by rogue nations, in spite of the fact that we presently have the best deterrent—our ICBMs. Any incoming ballistic missile can be easily tracked back to its source, making the launching nation wide open to any level of retaliation. The Clinton administration has deferred building a national missile defense system on the basis that there is no current threat, deciding instead that research and development should proceed to the point of being able to mount an initial defense in three years. And note that the simplest and most economical way for a nation to attack the US would be the introduce, clandestinely, any of the weapons of mass destruction by ship or simply use a truck, as was done in the Twin Towers attack in New York. Note that the best deterrent of a nuclear missile attack is the capability for a missile counterattack.

The US and the Soviets—and now the Russians—have relied on this for twenty-seven years, with the vital ABM Treaty. A rogue nuclear missile nation should be deterred, particularly if it were informed that for each incoming missile the US would retaliate with 10, 20, or 30 nuclear-tipped missiles. Just ten megaton missile bursts should virtually obliterate a rogue-led nation. (Assuring that the inhabitants get the message they should work to deter or destabilize their leader).

No doubt, a fortune could be saved by the US by using this technique. Should the US proceed it would scuttle the ABM Treaty, thereby derailing ongoing arms reductions—one of the most significant prevention actions ever. Further, as of this writing the Chinese are upset with the US for proceeding to provide missile defense for other nations, particularly Taiwan, and for boxing in China with a "containment strategy." What is urgently needed is an ABM Treaty with all nations having or planning a long-range missile capability.

In May, 1998 the Department of Defense awarded a $5 billion contract with Boeing to develop the missile defense system. There was no concomitant announcement from State/Arms Control and Disarmament Agency (ACDA) reassuring other nations as to its purportedly limited purpose. Had it done so, several nations will rethink their situations or go one step further and begin acquiring more missiles. Any arms reductions in the works would be affected. Several mini-arms races could well develop, triggered by US action.

Yes, here we are, working with the Russians to reduce nuclear weapons, including ICBMs, while at the same time taking steps—again—toward a missile defense, no doubt interpreted by Russia as a violation of the ABM treaty and upsetting the offense-defense equation. Antithetical, yes? (Recall my argument: offense begets defense and vice versa). It just occurred to me that the Boeing contract was let on the day following the Senate vote to expand NATO eastward, which is interpreted by some groups in Moscow as threatening. We will see how Russia reacts to this double-whammy.

President Gorbachev gave a talk in Moscow February 17, 1987 before a world-wide audience, a talk which could shed light on current actions. He said, "Now I would like to talk about passions which flared up in recent days about the deployment of a first phase of SDI [US missile defense]. . . . The aim is clearly to blast the [ABM] Treaty. From the start the political and philosophical essence . . . was to ensure stability due to the absence of anti-missile defense and in this way and the eternal competition between the sword and the shield, which is particularly dangerous in a nuclear age. . . . today, however, they [the US] want to remove that crucial brake in the way of the arms race.

"When the Treaty[ABM] is annulled, the nuclear missile race will acquire new dimensions and will be complemented by the arms race in outer space . . . By undermining the ABM Treaty the US Administration scorns the pledge and the signature of the United States put to a Treaty 15 years ago."

He went on to support international law banning deployment of any weapons of mass destruction in space. Then he added . . . "the development continues of more powerful and sophisticated weapons which are cynically called exotic.

"The uniqueness . . . of the situation is emphasized by the threat of the arms race spreading into space. If this happened the very idea of arms control would be compromised . . . Destabilization would become reality and be fraught with crisis. The risk of accidental breakout of the war would increase by several orders."

"In November 1985 President Reagan and I made the following pledge in Geneva: 'to prevent an arms race in space and to terminate it on earth.'"

The new, incipient missile defense program, aimed at defending against rogue-led nations will, no doubt alienate Russia. If the US pushes too hard it could well push the Russians backward into a political system reminiscent of the old Communist system. Their DUMA (the lower house of the congress) is loaded with card-carrying communists who would relish moving backward politically.

The Cold War and the arms race are over. Thanks to Presidents Gorbachev and Yeltsin, Russia has moved into a democracy-of-sorts and, a market economy, though they are still struggling. US policy today should be to do everything in its power to aid and assist Russia to succeed. The US, waving the new "missile defense" flag, is like waving a red flag in front of a bull. This on top of NATO pushing eastward, in my view, was like poking a finger in Russia's eye—and with more expansion yet to come. Instead, why not bring Russia into NATO as a full member, rather than its present nonvoting role?

Once again, deploying missile defense weapons—just as piling on offensive weapons—starts an arms races. Will the US unsettle and destabilize the world—or will it take the high road, be the world leader in striving to prevent conflicts? While writing this, Russia is at odds with NATO over the Kosovo conflict. Russia must be feeling like an outcast. Still another reason for bringing Russia in as a full-fledged member of NATO.

Yes, Star Wars is newly alive and kicking. Only it's now called merely "missile defense," ostensibly to defend against rogue-led nations. The following is an OP-ED piece, titled "Missile Defense Debunked," which I wrote for the Washington Post in March, 1999:

> "With the Senate's 97-3 vote, both houses of congress are on the let's have a missile defense bandwagon. President Clinton, too, is on the bandwagon, as he dropped his veto threat; earlier he had hedged his position by directing the development of missile defense to the point of having the capability within three years. It's deja vu, having spent more than $50 billion on Star Wars missile defense research—with no usable product to show. And, to this day, no tests have been successful. The Military-Industrial Complex must be jubilant while President Eisenhower is turning over in his grave. Yes, missile defense sounds great—on the surface. But . . . ?

"Two nations are quite upset about it: Russia and China. Prime Minister Primikov yelled "foul," witnessing the US again violating a sacred treaty, the US-Soviet Anti-Ballistic Treaty, in force and effective for twenty-seven years, having prevented the game of adding defense, prompting more offense, then more defense, etc., ad infinitum. Without that treaty the US and the Soviets/Russians might still be building more intercontinental missiles and defense systems—at our taxpayers expense. The last nuclear arms race cost the US $13 trillion. Should the US proceed, the Russians could well reverse ongoing arms reductions with US, by delaying or scrapping START II, now awaiting the Russian DUMA's OK, and which Primikov has been promoting—up to now.

"China is protesting the US supplying missile defense in Taiwan and Japan, claiming the US is inaugurating a new containment policy in the Far East. The beginning of still another arms race.

"Who in Washington is arguing the case for prevention? The State Department and its Arms Control and Disarmament Agency haven't been heard from. There are number of steps that they could be taking by selling the president on:

1. Entering dialogue with the six—or so—rogue-led nations with the view of their forgoing long-range missiles. A selling point: make it clear that, if used, the US would retaliate many-fold (a few nuclear weapons could essentially destroy those small nations).
2. Instead of scrapping the ABM treaty with the Russians, convene all capable nations with the view of obtaining a World Anti-Ballistic Treaty.

Are we taxpayers going to sit on our hands while our national leaders foster arms races, squander billions of our dollars, and make the US and the world a more dangerous place?

It is, indeed, deja vu."

Another Way

In any event, a rogue-led nation bent on attacking the US has a wide choice, other than missiles. It could obtain a small nuclear weapon, such as a suitcase neutron bomb, which could wipe out much of a major city—or kill many with a chemical or biological weapon delivered surreptitiously. Though these threats are high on the administration's do list, it's not yet apparent what it is doing about them.

So now we have these rogue threats as well as the possibility of slowed or stopped arms reductions with the Russians. Once again primordial fear takes hold, governing our actions.

At a minimum, why not sit down face-to-face with the rogue leaders to discern their logic and thinking, and to state our views, to outline a future as proposed here. Isn't there an adage: "Know thine enemy?"

Another Incipient Arms Race

In May, 1998 India suddenly conducted five underground nuclear weapons tests. True to form, India, fearful of its neighbor Pakistan, took the first step; it is that first step that starts an arms race. Of course Pakistan felt obliged to match the five tests and with a small touch of one-upmanship, detonated a sixth. Obviously, there had been insufficient communication between the two nations and insufficient preventive action by the international community. No doubt India thought it had weighed the consequences before acting, but, clearly, it hadn't considered the history of the birth and life of arms races. India hadn't learned from the US-Soviet experience—the start and the ensuing actions in their nuclear arms race; having spent trillions of dollars in building nuclear weapons and their delivery systems, they finally concluded that there can be no winner, and for years now the two nations have been working diligently, if slowly, at destroying their nuclear weapons. India, sadly, is a nation in dire need of resources to boost the standard of living of its people!

Much had transpired prior to nuclear tests. The US apparently had aided India's military solution by providing it nuclear technology, as well as providing missile technology to China, India's avowed potential enemy. A Congressional investigation of the Clinton administration's role in supplying this aid has been started to determine its legality. Pakistan received its nuclear know-how from China.

After the tests, the US, Japan, Canada, Australia and Germany applied sanctions, actions which had to have been weighed by India before starting the tests. Several other nations, such as Russia, France, and Britain chose not to join in applying sanctions. While sanctions may have some effect on the two participants, they acted knowing the probable result. The impact of economic sanctions on India and Pakistan is upon the people, not their leaders. And those who apply sanctions can be cutting off their own noses, for instance Boeing may lose a contract for airliners with India, which could be picked up by a US ally, as happened when the French stepped in, selling the Airbus to Iran. Within two weeks of the event India's stock market dropped 15%.

At the heart of the issue was Kashmir, over which India and Pakistan have fought twice in their three wars over many years. (Recall that, when I was representing the US at the SEATO Military Staff Planners' Conference in Hawaii on Vietnam way back in the 1960s, even then the focus kept reverting back to the antipathy between India and Pakistani representatives).

Several people have proposed steps to be taken on the heel of the dual nuclear weapons tests. Senator McCain suggests an agreement between the two nations not to test further; proposes mediation of the Kashmir issue; and suggests a US Security guarantee. Senator Kerry proposes that they agree not to weaponize the nuclear test devices. He suggested that the UN Security Council come together and that treaties won't do it.

Zalmay Khalilzad, the Director of Strategic Studies at RAND and former Assistant Under Secretary of Defense Policy Planning in the Bush administration, made several cogent proposals:

"1. Washington should seek an agreement between India and Pakistan not to produce or stockpile weapons. An agreement by both countries to join the Nuclear Test Ban Treaty is not enough.

2. . . . the US should take the lead in organizing a broader meeting involving India, Pakistan and the permanent members of the UN Security Council for the purpose of developing a broader regional security architecture that would address the issue of nuclear weapons.

3. . . . the US must focus on steps that would address the likelihood of conflict between the two nations, including confidence building measures and seeking to resolve disputes such as the Kashmir issue. . . .

4. . . . the US needs to strengthen both its intelligence and defense efforts to deal with the increasing danger of the spread of nuclear

weapons. . . . Investing in increased capability for locating nuclear weapons any where in the world . . . and for redoubling our efforts with regard to missile defense."[3]

A few weeks later the foreign secretaries of the Big Five nations met in Geneva to review the situation, mulling over what rewards should be considered but concerned that this would encourage other nations to follow the lead of India and Pakistan.

Then on June 6, the Associated Press reported "The 15 members of the Security Council demanded in a unanimous vote that India and Pakistan refrain from further nuclear tests, halt weapons programs and sign nuclear control agreements unconditionally. The response could have been anticipated. The Indian Foreign Ministry denounced the resolution as 'coercive and unhelpful' and said 'we find it grotesque that an organ of the United Nations should seek to address India in this manner.' "

Pakistan's UN ambassador, Ahmad Kamak, accused major powers of using nuclear treaties "to legitimize their own possessions of huge nuclear arsenals . . . in perpetuity and as a blunt instrument" to deny then to others.

"Other non-nuclear states, including Canada, also sent a strong message to the United States and the other four nuclear powers, telling them to fulfill commitments to reduce their own nuclear arsenals.

"The message points to the challenge facing the nuclear powers—the United states, Russia. China, France and Britain—in marshaling international pressure to curb the nuclear arms race in South Asia.

"Japanese Ambassador Hishashi Owada said the Indian and Pakistani tests last month threatened the entire global system of nuclear controls and could plunge the international community 'into an uncontrollable world of nuclear proliferation.' "[4]

To compound the problem, in April, 1999 India test fired a new nuclear capable missile which could hit any target in Pakistan.

---

[3]"The Nuclear Subcontinent,"The Wall Street Journal, May 20, 1998, republished by permission of the Wall Street Journal, Copyright 1998, Dow Jones & Company, Inc. All rights reserved.

[4]The Charlottesville,Va."Daily Progress", 6-6-98, by the Associated Press.

So, out of this situation come two issues of great enormity. It is crystal clear that the lesser and wannabe nuclear powers will ignore demands for nuclear reduction, cessation, and abstinence until all the nuclear powers get serious about their reduction and elimination of nuclear weapons. The other issue addresses the matter of preventing the India-Pakistan-type situations from occurring in the first place. Yes, the above ideas by the post-event quarterbacks are useful—save Khalilzad's notion of redoubling missile defense (covered later in this chapter)—but they are all after the fact. Now, the problem is how to put the horse back in the barn and keep it there.

What interests me keenly is preventing controversies which have the potential of erupting into overt peace-breaking action. In this century there have been more than 250 wars, not to mention the countless squabbles between nations. These, and international peacekeeping operations which at times involve neighboring nations, crop up with clock-like regularity. One would think, with all the treaties, the efforts of the UN Secretary-General, the UN General Assembly, the Security Council, other international bodies, and coalitions, as well as individual nations, that such happenings would have been prevented. Obviously not.

A Watch Group

Here's my proposal for resolving serious altercations between nations, for preventing their use of force. It is the mission of the Security Council to "determine the existence of any threat to the peace, breach of the peace, or act of aggression and shall make recommendations, or decide what measures shall be taken. . . . " Any nation having a security problem with a neighbor has access to the President of the Security Council and through any of its fifteen members. Conversely, the Security Council can intervene in such situations under its own authority.

But take a case like that of India-Pakistan. If, early on, their differences were presented to the Security Council by either or both nations, or by a third party, or even initiated by the Security Council itself, the Council could designate a panel of several nations, a 'Watch Group', to investigate, report, and to act as moderators or mediators, then to recommend specific actions—and to stay in constant touch with the parties until the differences are resolved, whereupon the Watch Group would be disbanded. The selection of Watch Group members would require special care. No doubt each situation will dictate unique handling by Security Council. In time, there would likely be many Watch Groups working simultaneously.

The advantages of the Watch Group over present methods and techniques are several. Currently, perforce, individual nations give attention only spasmodically to the difficulties of other nations. Each has its own self-serving agenda: aligning nations into its camp, fostering bilateral-lateral trade, selling weapons, providing—or not—sensitive information and equipment to selected clients, and unilateral or allies' use of sanctions, etc. The Watch Group, with its multilateral approach, could be expected to avoid many of these entanglements—as should the fifteen-nation Security Council.

Effective use of this kind of technique could save much in terms of lives and treasure—and could just prevent another war—even a war of mass destruction—or another world war.

Nuke the Nukes

When working on the WW III war plan in the '50s I hadn't a second thought about our growing nuclear arsenal. After all, the Air Force had a virtual world monopoly, a powerful deterrent. In the early '80s, though, retired from the Air Force, it finally sank in that nukes were unusable and that both sides were squandering immense resources—in the trillions of dollars—in a lose-lose situation and, in our case contributing to the trebling of our national debt to $5.5 trillion in the '80s.

The Cuban missile crisis was a wake up call. Secretary of Defense McNamara was in the oval office in October 1962 at the time, and later reminisced that "We came within a hair's breadth of nuclear war." Hundreds of nuclear weapons could be enroute in a matter of minutes. A national leader would have only minutes to make the decision to unleash them. And once started there is no assured way to end it. Worse is the thought that civilization could end because of a false or misinterpreted reading on the radar scopes, or an erroneous communication to or from the nation's head, or by a simple electrical malfunction.

Don't take any solace from the announcement a few years ago that the we and the Russians no longer target each other—as it takes only seconds to retarget the intercontinental missiles. There is no such agreement with China.

What would our Creator think—after putting in several millions of years bringing us this far? Would He just give up the notion of *Homo sapiens*—now *Homo destructus?* Now there is the need for hundreds of billions dollars more to clean up the nuclear contamination caused by our frenzied building of them—contamination, for example, of the Colorado River water, Los Angeles' source of drinking water. As of this late juncture there is still no known safe, long term method of containing nuclear materials. Only recently our government announced the creation of a large underground storage facility for fissile material in Arizona , but there is no finite information on how long it will remain contained.

In the early days we were told that nukes would reduce the need for conventional weapons, yet for years we have spent money on both, lavishly.

Transparency

As national security is a nation's number one concern, the reduction of weapons of mass destruction requires a considerable measure of faith in the process—in addition to international inspection of the process. Here's a thought which could ease concerns and facilitate the actual destruction of weapons: televise internationally the actual destruction of the delivery vehicles.

I visualize scenes on millions of TVs around the world of the actual destruction of US and Russian ICBMs on a split-screen, each screen displaying a box score of the numbers of each type destroyed and the numbers remaining to reach zero, the numbers changing after each event. The methods of destruction could vary by type of weapon, but the sight of high explosive charges destroying the delivery vehicle or the mashing of the vehicles would be impressive. Commentators would fill in the history of arms reduction and its future. I see the leaders of the nations involved making live statements citing the critical importance of the occasion and the cooperation between nations. Too, I visualize the inspection teams expounding on their role, as well as the safe handling and storage of the fissionable material.

These scenes would be repeated as more weapons delivery vehicles are readied. The entire world would not only be fascinated by the spectacle but greatly relieved to actually see peace gaining ground, the threat of annihilation receding, and millions people eagerly awaiting the next show.

Does this more than half-century of a fantastically dangerous, expensive and potentially terminal roller coaster ride suggest that there may be a different, better way to conduct world affairs? Doesn't it seem like the US Military-Industrial Complex is winning another inning—if not the ball game.

The Arms Control and Disarmament

The Arms Control and Disarmament Agency (ACDA) has had the difficult job of orchestrating arms reductions. In the Fall of 1997 the administration decided to move ACDA into the State Department, an act of considerable importance, as will be noted later. ACDA's job requires that it work with former or current "enemies" of the United States on the most sensitive issues any nation can have, its national security and its very survival. Its work just may be the most critical of any Washington agency.

In a lecture in the Fall of 1997 at the Miller Center of Public Affairs, University of Virginia, by a member of ACDA, the speaker indicated that his organization is not only being merged, but submerged in the bowels of the State Department. In my view this is a gross mistake, as I see the ACDA function as the heart of the pre-vention work that needs to be done. For these reasons I think it should be kept virtually intact in the State Department or better, as an inde-pendent agency. Its name should be changed to: The Arms Control, Disarmament and *Prevention* Agency—for reasons that follow.

Usually progress in obtaining arms control agreements is stymied until a prior stage is approved, such as waiting for ratifica-tion by the Senate, or the equivalent body in other nations. Reduc-tion of nuclear of weapons is but one ACDA's many concerns.

In addition to nuclear weapons, the ACDA has negotiated and monitors the Non-Proliferation Treaty (NPT), Chemical Weapons Convention (CWC), Biological Weapons (BWC), Conventional Forces in Europe (CFET), and the Comprehensive Test Ban Treaty (CTBT) in work, which needs a number of signatories—India hav-ing already announced it will not ratify—and Land Mines, which the United States has not signed. In all, a large plate.

Treaty overload is a special problem. There are a number of treaties lined up to be ratified by the Senate. John Rhinelander, Vice Chairman of the Arms Control Association put it this way: ". . . there may be as many as eight to ten treaties during the second Clinton second term. . . . There are four or five treaties that will probably come up during the second Clinton administration, and I think they have no chance of getting through the Senate. They include two nuclear-free-zone treaties. . . . Then we have the Conventional Forces in Europe (CFE) Treaty . . . START ll is another . . . Finally you have the BWC, not yet even negotiated. . . . In summary, if we don't get the CWC and START ll, then we will have arms control really going into deep freeze, and that is going to adversely affect relations."[5] Note: the Senate did ratify START ll, but its ratification by the Russian DUMA may be a long time coming, leaving strategic arms reductions indefinitely stalled.

At the current pace, with existing weapons and the new weapons systems coming along and because of the environment in which it works, I see ACDA as always behind the power curve (an airman's term for stalling and losing control of an airplane). In other

---

[5]John Rhinelander, Arms Control Today, Arms Control Association, March, 1997, 1726 M Street, Suite 201, Washington, D.C. 20036.

words, using currently available means it can never catch up, it will always be snowed under with cumulating new problems, new work, ponderous negotiations—in the most difficult work-environment ever, and with the most important issues ever. Granted, in the final analysis it is politics that determine the pace of arms agreements. And I have yet to even mention prevention.

A New Way: Fast Track.

As the use of treaties to control and reduce arms is unacceptably slow, a bit of research opened up a way to put them on a Fast Track. Here I am, back to matters of law, this time a new and different look at the law, at Executive Agreements, in the "Congressional Quarterly, Guide to the Presidency, 1989," quoted below.

Article ll, section 2, clause 2 of the Constitution declares that "the president shall have the Power, by and with the Advice and Consent of the Senate, to make treaties, provided two thirds of the Senators present concur. . . ." The Congressional Quarterly goes on, "Nevertheless, the executive branch has established itself as the dominant branch in treaty making.

"An executive agreement is a pact other than a treaty made by the president or representative of the president with a foreign leader or government. . . . The president can make agreements with foreign governments without congressional consent. . . . Contemporary presidents can accomplish virtually anything through an executive agreement that can be accomplished through a treaty . . . The use of executive agreements has grown dramatically in the twentieth century . . . the Supreme Court has repeatedly upheld the President's power to make international agreements without the consent of the Senate.

"When the Senate refused to approve the treaty of President Theodore Roosevelt and the Dominican Republic Roosevelt continued the arrangement under the executive agreement. . . . Executive agreements were used to expand the NATO Treaty."

An effort was made in Congress in the 1950's (the Bricker Amendment) to radically alter the way the United States enters into agreements to, in part, make the treaty effective "only through the enactment of appropriate legislation by the Congress." The amendment was not enacted.[6]

In our current situation most arms control and disarmament measures are designed to limit or reduce weapons in concert with another nation or, in the future, with several nations concurrently. The policy of incremental reduction has been established; the Senate has been participating in a concept of building upon a framework through ratification. Precious time is wasted by the Senate requiring ratification of every step in the reduction process. Each reduction reduces the threat to the United States, even from annihilation.

The President, as head the executive branch of the government, is recognized as the dominant branch in treaty making. Precedents show his right to use presidential Executive Agreements in this regard in spite of Congressional direction to the contrary. A reasoned appeal to the Senate would be helpful; he has powerful arguments for Fast Track. Speed is of the essence, which can be attained by putting these agreements on the Fast Track of Executive Agreements. Fast Track should speed the entire reduction and elimination process—pare years off the time to complete the reduction process. The American people would be solidly behind the president.

That Ounce of Prevention
(Now worth tons of cure)

Which nation would wish to repeat the scenario of the last fifty years? Will it take a sledgehammer over our heads to prevent this kind of world-wide, fear-based one-upmanship? Even more destructive weapons are in the works. Will we let it happen all over again— even before cleaning up after the last arms race?

After several million years it is time to conquer fear, to outlaw new weapons of mass destruction, to take a new course. Past and present techniques for harnessing ever-increasingly destructive weapons have not even come close to a solution. Implementing and enforcing worldwide Rule of Law is a significant part of the answer.

---

[6] Congressional Quarterly, Guide to the Presidency, 1989.

Space

According to an editorial by John T. Correll in the Air Force Magazine of March 1996, he reported that in January 1996 the Air Force conducted a comprehensive study by the Air Force Scientific Advisory Board, "New World Vistas" focused on aero-space technology options that are likely to emerge in the 21st century, all in preparation for the 1997 DOD Quadrennial Review.

He stated "Some of the assessments in the 'New World Vistas' have a ring of inevitability. One such is the prediction that space will become vastly more important as a 'domain of conflict'. . . . Control of space will become critical during the next decade, the report says. That entails protecting our own space assets—possibly with directed energy weapons—and denying use of space to others. The Pentagon did not publish papers done by the 'Vistas' study panels, but one of them leaked to the press, explored the sobering implications of space as a domain of conflict. The study said the application of force from space will become feasible and affordable within thirty years and that it would then be possible to complete the equivalent of a Desert Storm strategic air campaign in a matter of hours. . . . Our future enemies, who ever they may be, will obtain knowledge and weapons better than those we have at present by making rather small investments. . . . The studies thus far indicate that we are driven forward by technology and need on three fronts: global awareness, global mobility, and the projection of lethal power."[7]

In the October, 1996 issue of Air Force Magazine Editor Correll wrote another editorial "The Command of Space," stating "More than anything else, it was the Persian Gulf War that finally brought recognition and respect. Satellites were everywhere, doing almost everything. . . . The Air Force has begun to prepare carefully for the eventuality that military operations—and probably combat—are going to occur in space . . . some twenty nations will have space-based capabilities by 2000."

[7]Air Force Magazine, Editor Correll, March, 1996 , author of "New World Vistas," Reprinted by permission from Air Force Magazine, Published by the Air Force Association.

Correll identifies " . . . two 'new' military missions in space that bid to drive doctrinal change over the next ten to twenty-five years:

- Space force application is military action in space with a direct effect on Earth . . .
- Space and space control means the protecting our ability to use force, presumably adversaries from interfering with that use, and negating an adversary's ability to exploit its own space forces."

" 'Undoubtedly, the most provocative subject in any discussion of the future of space is the subject of weapons and the likelihood of the use,' says Gen. Thomas S. Moorman, Jr., Air Force Vice Chief of Staff, a distinguished veteran of the space campaigns. 'Here, I am referring to the broadest categories: space based lasers to shoot down hostile ICBM's, space weapons that attack other satellites or weapons released from space platforms that destroy terrestrial targets. Today, these kinds of systems clearly break the current thresholds of acceptability and introduce Anti-ballistic Missile Treaty issues and social and political reservations. But the 21st century could well see a change. . . . That might happen because the necessity of everyday life and our economic and commercial interests have become so linked in space that we cannot allow an adversary to control it. . . .'"[8]

Then in the August, 1997 issue of Air Force Magazine, John A. Tirpak, a Senior Editor, wrote "The Rise of Space," in which he interviews Air Force Gen. Howell M. Estes, III [Commander of Air Force Space Command]. "A tremendous amount of our economic strength is migrating to space. . . . Within a decade . . . government agencies and private concerns are 'going to put 1800 satellites into orbit,' valued at a trillion dollars or more. . . . Dependence on these satellites, according to the General, will represent a target too tempting to an enemy. . . . 'Then an attack comes,' he added, 'we as a

[8]Air Force Magazine Editor Correll , "The Command in Space," October, 1996, Reprinted by permission from Air Force Magazine, Published by the Air Force Association.

nation are going to protect the investment.' Estes said, 'If we're ever going to do this thing, now is the time'. . . . and that there will be 'sharing in the development cost between the government and industry' . . . Asked to define space control, Estes offered an apology. If I said 'control of the air . . . you'd know exactly what I was talking about. [It means] I want to maintain superiority, ... operating freely, and denying that to the enemy. Just translate those words to space.' He defined space control as surveillance, deterrence, protection and negation . . . ironically most of the 'negation' concepts are terrestrial in nature . . .' He goes on, 'But just as armies were developed to protect land lines of communications, navies to protect the sea lines, and the air to protect air routes, 'the same thing is going to happen in space,' Estes maintained . . . 'and we may find one way to protect ourselves—to go to space to do it.' Likewise, despite treaties governing the emplacement of space based antiballistic missile systems, Estes feels that circumstances may change. The treaties are 'OK today,' said Estes, 'but I'll tell you, if those ballistic missiles threaten this country and that we find that space based weapons are the best means to defend against them, I'm sure the issue's going to be revisited.' If space offers 'the best way' to defend the nation, 'I think that we will make that decision.' Estes said, 'we're not going to leave our citizenry unprotected.' "

"Estes was asked why, when the Air Force leadership last fall elected to shift emphasis toward the 'space and air force,' that the name of the Air Force was not changed to 'Aerospace Force. . . . He replied that, for now, 'it was a bridge too far. . . . and that there may be a time when there is 'space' in our title.' "[9]

If I were in uniform, involved in space issues and the future of the Air Force, I would be doing the same things that General Estes has outlined. That's what he and all the service chiefs are paid for— to protect and defend the security of the United States. On the other hand, if a reasonably sure way were at hand to prevent the threatening of US interests in space I believe they would be at ease, knowing that they need not put their personnel in harms way.

[9] Air Force Magazine, John A. Tirpak, a Senior Editor, author of "The Rise of Space," August, 1997. Reprinted by permission from Air Force Magazine, Published by the Air Force Association.

In R. Jeffrey Smith's October 3, 1997 article, "In Initial Test, US Army to Fire Ground Laser at Air Force Satellite," he revealed the first planned test to destroy a satellite. It didn't take long for the Army to kick off another arms race—just talking about it. Secretary of Defense Cohen "approved the test while traveling in Europe." A clamor erupted. Even the director of the Satellite Industry Association, Clay Mowry, said, "executives of some 18 aerospace firms are worried that the test could set a dangerous precedent and promote development of lasers that ultimately could threaten commercial satellites now producing an estimated $23 billion in revenue annually." Kenneth Bacon, a Pentagon spokesman, emphasized that "it will violate no arms treaties or international agreements."[10] (That clinches the need to adhere strictly to the Anti-Ballistic Treaty with the Russians, tighten space treaties and protocols, e.g., the Moon/Outer Space Treaty addresses orbiting vehicles, but not stationary satellites, not to mention new international law). Several in Congress protested the test, some writing to the President. Apparently, the State Department was not informed. And doesn't this cry out for some inter-government controls over the development and test of weapons systems.

Isn't it becoming crystal clear that preventing conflict in space must be pursued with the greatest urgency!

In another piece by Air Force Magazine Editor Correll, in January 1996, he predicted that "space will become vastly more important as a domain of conflict." His prediction was on the mark, as his March 1999 article, "A Roadmap for Space," reveals. It starts, "If the Air Force follows the advice of its top science advisors, it could

---

[10] R. Jeffrey Smith's "In Initial Test, US Army to Fire Ground Laser at Air Force Satellite," **[Copyright 1997, The Washington Post, Reprinted with permission]**.

move swiftly toward a stronger position in space in the opening years
of the 21st Century." The core of scientists' advice centered on the
"ability to deliver militarily significant amounts of laser energy
through space to targets." And if the Air Force follows the advice of
its top science advisors, "it could move swiftly to toward a stronger
position in space in the opening years of the 21st Century."

The Chief Scientist of the Air Force, Dr. Daniel E. Hastings,
is quoted as visualizing "projecting laser energy from or through
space, meaning that some of the weapons might be located on the
ground."

Correll goes on, "The issue is complicated by the fact that deployment of a space-based laser, a prime use of which would be ballistic missile defense, is presently prohibited by the Anti-Ballistic
Missile[ABM] Treaty. On the other hand, there is strong support in
Congress for the space-based laser, and the last year's defense bill
called for on-orbit testing of a "readiness demonstrator" by 2005 or
very soon thereafter."

"The roadmap said that the current technology, a chemical laser
system designed in the 1979's, is not mature enough to support such
a demonstration and that "fixes" to the existing system will not bring
it up to snuff."

"The Scientific Advisory Board[SAB] recommended that the
Air Force not proceed with the readiness demonstrator test "at this
time." And [Dr.] Borky,[Vice Chairman of the SAB] emphasized
that the SAB's reservations are about the current technology, not the
desirability of the system . . . and that "directed energy from space,
whether generated in space or relayed from air or ground, will be a
major weapon capability in the next millennium . . ." (Underling
supplied). In December 1998, F. Whitten Peters, acting Secretary of
the Air Force. . . . said "The Air Force believes that it could reasonably try to deploy something in the 2010 time frame, and we are
working in that plan."

And finally, " the SAB said the Air Force should 'preserve the
option' to develop an Aerospace Operations Vehicle which could be
launched from Earth, fly through space at hypersonic speeds, and
perform its mission either from space or by reentering the atmosphere. . . . This would be consistent with the development of a corps

of aerospace war fighters, skilled in all dimensions of applying spaceborne and airborne instruments of national power."[11]

Preventive Measures

The State Department/Arms Control and Disarmament Agency, should already be coordinating with DOD, planning its preventive measures. By my review of the several space treaties, they are not adequate in view of recent technological developments. I should think that early on the State Department would convene all affected nations to review the complex issues—as a precursor to an early, badly needed updating of international space law.

Surely an arms race in space is already under way. No doubt, ·with all the publicity, other nations are making their plans. Granted, the US, as the most technologically adept nation could attain military advantage of sorts. But others will challenge and eventually assert themselves militarily.

In the early stages of the US-Soviet nuclear arms race neither nation foresaw a 55 year race or its monumental costs—to both sides. And now we struggle to reduce our nuclear arsenals, again at great cost and with no plan to eliminate the weapons that, still, can annihilate both nations—and maybe poison the rest of the world, at a minimum.

It would be the utmost folly and—stupidity—to start an arms race in space. Yes, the power exerted by the Military-Industrial Complex will be difficult to overcome, but our national leaders must look at the issues squarely and institute a major effort to avert a space arms race.

As the technological age marches forward, imperiling national security and degrading the economy, the more important it becomes to develop preventive measures to avoid military conflict, and the more important it is that agreements be sought with as many nations as possible.

[11]Air Force Magazine Editor Correll's, article, "A Roadmap for Space, "March 1998. Reprinted by permission from Air Force Magazine, Published by the Air Force Association.

Should we fall short, and conflict in space occurs, or missile defenses proliferate, or nuclear weapons are not eliminated, the President and the Secretary of State will be primarily responsible. Should the Congress delay or obstruct the strategy it, too, will share the responsibility.

Arms Reduction and Prevention Measures

I propose:

1. The presidents of the US and Russia meet to speed up the US-Russia reduction and elimination of nuclear weapons, their delivery systems and missile defenses using Fast Track, as the current rate of a few hundred a year is but a snail's pace. Most important, is the setting of a date for the destruction of the last nuclear weapon. Of course, the handling and disposal of nuclear material must be done with great care and accountability. The destruction of delivery vehicles is a matter of metal-bending, cutting or use of explosives. Worldwide public witness on TV of the destruction of delivery vehicles would have many salutary effects; using this technique public destruction could provide "reassurance" and confidence. Verification to be done by UNSCOM in all situations in Paras. 1-5.

2. At an early date, while keeping US missile defense on hold, meet with all nations having the capability to build or operate missiles and missile defense systems with the view to obtaining a world-wide Anti-Ballistic Missile Treaty outlawing them. Installing missile defenses will not only spawn a defensive arms race, but also sabotage offensive reductions, thereby halting the reduction of nuclear weapons, forestalling their elimination. Note that missile defense is closely related to the prevention of conflict in space.

3. Bring China, France and the United Kingdom into the nuclear weapon reduction process with the objective of reaching zero simultaneously with the US and Russia. The presidents of the US and Russia call and head the meeting (the Reagan-Gorbachev talks resulted in ending the Cold War).

4. Followed by the same agenda with Iran, Iraq, Libya, Israel, India, Pakistan and North Korea and other nations with the ability to develop or employ nuclear weapons.
5. Meet with the 25 nations that have or are working on nuclear, chemical or biological weapons to set elimination dates. (In November, 1997 Secretary of Defense Cohen announced that 25 nations possess or may be developing with the threat.) Note that early preventive measures would preclude also.
6. As the number of nuclear weapons approach zero, create a UN force—a prevention force—to deal with possible hidden nuclear or other weapons of mass destruction or use such weapons. Such force would consist of a number of ships with nuclear missiles at the ready, equipped with missile defense, manned with international crews, continuously at sea on random tracks as a deterrent as well as a counter-force. Awareness of such a force should discourage rogues from hiding or using such weapons.
7. Take the lead in creating international law prohibiting any new weapons of mass destruction by any concept, conceived or yet to be conceived, e.g. directed energy weapons.
8. Strengthen the international agency for the monitoring of all subsequent nuclear, biological and chemical (NBC) international agreements and any in the atmosphere and in space. (The current United Nations Special Commission (UNSCOM) could be the base or the umbrella organization for current monitors. UNSCOM is the agency that has been active in Iraq, monitoring weapons of mass destruction at the direction of the Security Council.)

The overall plan, the results of negotiations, and progress in destruction of weapons would be transparent at all times, giving all nations a sense of confidence and security.

A US Prevention/Reduction Management System

It is glaringly obvious that a new system is needed within the US government for controlling its own new weapons systems and their development and testing. It should be designed to support arms reduction and control negotiations; to prevent the start of another arms race; and most important to prevent armed conflict. Under the existing system the Department of Defense is charged with developing new weapons systems and strategies for the defense of the US. Its contractors, of course, are motivated by profit. The State Department and the Arms Control and Disarmament (and Prevention) Agency work in the realm of foreign policy and international relations. The State Department should be required, by law if necessary, to vet every new Defense Department's weapons system, concept and test as part of the decision-making process. The Defense Department's actions should not interfere with arms control and disarmament negotiations or plans. The President would have the final word. Preventing arms races and reductions in weapons should have a priority at least equal to if not exceeding that of the current sizing and shaping of the military forces.

Virtually every national security action taken by Defense and State needs to be coordinated. The test of a laser beam against one of our own satellites is a case in point. It could upset policy objectives or negotiations conducted by State/ACDA. For lack of coordination the test was canceled. The simple fact that Secretary Cohen placed a request for $1 billion to deal militarily with the twenty-five nations which have weapons of mass destruction. What should State be doing? Was the Defense action coordinated with State? What are the priorities?

No doubt, the Defense Department would quarrel with this constraint on its freedom of action but they would have the opportunity to present their case to the President. No doubt the Congress will want to be informed.

And why not an international clearing house for all new weapons systems, including testing? This is not as radical an idea as it might seem. It could separate the law-abiding from rogue-led nations.

State/ACDA should be overjoyed creating preventive measures, while cleaning up this century's mess. I wish them a running start and great success.

Again, the issue here is the prevention of another devastating (I use this word for lack of a stronger one) arms race and lesser conflicts—as well as recovering from the last arms race. The US started a nuclear arms race that was ongoing for nearly fifty years, with many more years to eliminate nuclear weapons—if we follow past approaches. With the innovations proposed here the reduction period can be expedited considerably. Some ideas and suggestions are made here; certainly others will be developed. The key is to focus on preventing the emergence of new arms races. Any nation, the United States included, should be precluded from starting one anew. The byword must be prevention, prevention, prevention!

For background on nuclear arms and other treaties and negotiations, I've included the following from the The World Almanac and Book of Facts, 1999

"Aug. 5, 1963—Limited Test Ban Treaty signed in Moscow by the US, USSR, and Great Britain; prohibited testing of nuclear weapons in space, above ground, and under water.

Jan. 27, 1967—Outer Space Treaty banned the introduction of nuclear weapons and other weapons of mass destruction into space.

July 1, 1968—Nuclear Nonproliferation Treaty, with US, USSR, and Great Britain as major signers, limited the spread of military nuclear technology by agreement not to assist nonnuclear nations in getting or making nuclear weapons.

May 26, 1972—Strategic Arms Limitation Treaty (SALT I)—interim agreement—signed in Moscow by US and USSR. The treaty imposed a 5-year freeze on testing and deployment of intercontinental ballistic missiles (ICBMs) and submarine-launched ballistic missiles (SLBMs). An interim short-term agreement putting a ceiling on numbers of offensive nuclear weapons was also signed. SALT I was in effect until Oct. 3, 1977. In the area of defensive nuclear weapons, the separate ABM Treaty limited antiballistic missiles to 2 sites of 100 antiballistic missile launchers in each country (amended in 1974 to one site in each country).

July 3, 1974—ABM Treaty Revision (protocol on antiballistic missile systems) and Threshold Test Ban Treaty on limiting underground testing of nuclear weapons to 150 kilotons were signed by US and USSR in Moscow.

Sept. 1977—US and USSR agreed to continue to abide by SALT I, despite its expiration date.

June 18, 1979—SALT II, signed in Vienna by the US and USSR, constrained offensive nuclear weapons, limiting each side to 2,400 missile launchers and heavy bombers with that ceiling to apply until Jan. 1, 1985.

The treaty also set a subceiling of 1,320 ICBMs and SLBMs with multiple warheads on each side. Although approved by the US Senate Foreign Relations Committee, the treaty never reached the Senate floor for ratification because Pres. Jimmy Carter withdrew his support for the treaty following the Dec. 1979 invasion of Afghanistan by Soviet troops.

Dec.8, 1987—Intermediate-Range Nuclear Forces (INF) Treaty signed in Washington, D.C., by USSR leader Mikhail Gorbachev and US Pres. Ronald Reagan, eliminating all medium- and shorter-range nuclear missiles from Europe; ratified with conditions by US Senate on May 27, 1988.

July 31, 1991—Strategic Arms Reduction Treaty (START I) signed in Moscow by Soviet Pres. Mikhail Gorbachev and US Pres. George Bush to reduce strategic offensive arms by approximately 30 percent in three phases over seven years. START I was the first treaty to mandate reductions by the superpowers. The treaty was approved by the US Senate Oct. 1, 1992. With the breakup of the Soviet Union in December 1991, four former Soviet republics became independent nations with strategic nuclear weapons on their territory—Russia, Ukraine, Kazakhstan, and Belarus. The last 3 agreed in principle in 1992 to transfer their nuclear weapons to Russia and ratify START I. The Russian Supreme Soviet voted to ratify Nov. 4, 1992, but Russia decided not to provide the instruments of ratification until Ukraine, Kazakhstan, and Belarus each ratified START I and acceded to the Nuclear Nonproliferation Treaty (NPT) as nonnuclear nations. By late 1993, Belarus and Kazakhstan had ratified START I and acceded to the nonproliferation treaty. In February 1994, Ukraine ratified START II, but it had not yet acceded to the NPT.

Jan. 3, 1993—START II signed in Moscow by US Pres. George Bush and Russian Pres. Boris Yeltsin. Potentially the broadest disarmament pact in history, it called for both sides to reduce their long-range nuclear arsenals to about one-third of their then-current levels within a decade and would entirely eliminate land-based multiple-warhead missiles. Action will not be taken on START II until START I enters into force. START II will require ratification only by the US Senate and the legislature of Russia, which would, under the guidelines for START I finalization, be the only remaining nuclear republic of the former Soviet Union.

Aug. 5, 1963—Limited Test Ban Treaty signed in Moscow by the US, USSR, and Great Britain; prohibited testing of nuclear weapons in space, above ground, and under water.

Jan. 27, 1967—Outer Space Treaty banned the introduction of nuclear weapons and other weapons of mass destruction into space.

July 1, 1968—Nuclear Nonproliferation Treaty, with US, USSR, and Great Britain as major signers, limited the spread of military nuclear technology by agreement not to assist nonnuclear nations in getting or making nuclear weapons.

May 26, 1972—Strategic Arms Limitation Treaty (SALT I)—interim agreement—signed in Moscow by US and USSR. The treaty imposed a 5-year freeze on testing and deployment of intercontinental ballistic missiles (ICBMs) and submarine-launched ballistic missiles (SLBMs). An interim short-term agreement putting a ceiling on numbers of offensive nuclear weapons was also signed. SALT I was in effect until Oct. 3, 1977. In the area of defensive nuclear weapons, the separate ABM Treaty limited antiballistic missiles to 2 sites of 100 antiballistic missile launchers in each country (amended in 1974 to one site in each country).

July 3, 1974—ABM Treaty Revision (protocol on antiballistic missile systems) and Threshold Test Ban Treaty on limiting underground testing of nuclear weapons to 150 kilotons were signed by US and USSR in Moscow.

Sept. 1977—US and USSR agreed to continue to abide by SALT I, despite its expiration date.

June 18, 1979—SALT II, signed in Vienna by the US and USSR, constrained offensive nuclear weapons, limiting each side to 2,400 missile launchers and heavy bombers with that ceiling to apply until Jan. 1, 1985. The treaty also set a subceiling of 1,320 ICBMs and SLBMs with multiple warheads on each side. Although approved by the US Senate Foreign Relations Committee, the treaty never reached the Senate floor for ratification because Pres. Jimmy Carter withdrew his support for the treaty following the Dec. 1979 invasion of Afghanistan by Soviet troops.

Dec. 8, 1987—Intermediate-Range Nuclear Forces (INF) Treaty signed in Washington, D.C., by USSR leader Mikhail Gorbachev and US Pres. Ronald Reagan, eliminating all medium- and shorter-range nuclear missiles from Europe; ratified with conditions by US Senate on May 27, 1988.

July 31, 1991—Strategic Arms Reduction Treaty (START I) signed in Moscow by Soviet Pres. Mikhail Gorbachev and US Pres. George Bush to reduce strategic offensive arms by approximately 30 percent in three phases over seven years. START I was the first treaty to mandate reductions by the superpowers. The treaty was approved by the US Senate Oct. 1, 1992. With the breakup of the Soviet Union in December 1991, four former Soviet republics became independent nations with strategic nuclear weapons on their territory—Russia, Ukraine, Kazakhstan, and Belarus.

The last 3 agreed in principle in 1992 to transfer their nuclear weapons to Russia and ratify START I. The Russian Supreme Soviet voted to ratify Nov. 4, 1992, but Russia decided not to provide the instruments of ratification until Ukraine, Kazakhstan, and Belarus each ratified START I and acceded to the Nuclear Nonproliferation Treaty (NPT) as nonnuclear nations. By late 1993, Belarus and Kazakhstan had ratified START I and acceded to the nonproliferation treaty. In February 1994, Ukraine ratified START II, but it had not yet acceded to the NPT.

Jan. 3, 1993—START II signed in Moscow by US Pres. George Bush and Russian Pres. Boris Yeltsin. Potentially the broadest disarmament pact in history, it called for both sides to reduce their long-range nuclear arsenals to about one-third of their then-current levels within a decade and would entirely eliminate land-based multiple-warhead missiles. Action will not be taken on START II until START I enters into force. START II will require ratification only by the US Senate and the legislature of Russia, which would, under the guidelines for START I finalization, be the only remaining nuclear republic of the former Soviet Union. Start ll was ratified by the Senate in 1997.[12]

[12] Excerpts from the World Almanac and Book of Facts 1999, copyright 1998 by PRIMEDIA Reference Inc., One International Boulevard, Suite 444, Mahwah, NJ 07495-0017.

14

"BUD-NIPPING"

LESSONS FROM WW I & II

Recall in Part 1, my observations about nipping aggression in the bud: they were in those early days—the 50's—national war planning in the Air Staff in the Pentagon. Routinely, we were privy to State Department message traffic having to do with military matters from around the world. It didn't take long until a common thread emerged: if a small military action wasn't quickly quashed it would continue to fester and grow. It was then that the notion of "bud-nipping" entered my mind—and has remained.

Soon after the idea of this book germinated, the thought of looking back into history, emerged. Were there any "bud-nipping" situations which could be applied to today's situations?

World War I offers no clear "bud" but its aftermath set the stage for one. While on WW I, though, note the entangling alliances wherein Germany and Austria-Hungary were linked, as were France and Russia, with Britain in a loose alliance with France. This picture will play into a later chapter on Rule of Law. Recall that it was the assassination of Serbian Archduke Ferdinand and his wife by a boy of 19 that lit the fuse of WW I. Six days later, five empires were at war, (On the fifth day Adolph Hitler, an Austrian, petitioned the King of Bavaria for permission to enlist in a Bavarian regiment). Contrast this scene with today's Europe—with NATO, European Union and USCE.

On January 28, 1919 the Treaty of Versailles was signed by Germany and twenty-seven allied and associated powers. By its terms Germany was to disband its army, navy and air force. It was forbidden to fortify the Rhineland, a tiny buffer state between France and Germany, or to position arms there.

Hitler's Bud

Adolph Hitler, an ex-corporal, became Chancellor of the German Republic in 1933, starting the Nazi Revolution. State governments lost power. All offices were limited to Aryans. Summary executions and concentration camps appeared. The National Socialist Party became the sole party. Japan and Germany left the League of Nations in October, 1933, within three years of its creation in 1930. Hitler bolted the Versailles Treaty arms limitations, and decreed universal conscription. In March, 1935 he announced to the world that he was proceeding with compulsory military training and creating a new German Air Force—in violation of the Treaty.

Hitler tested his strength on March 7, 1936 by ordering three battalions into the forbidden Rhineland. The battalions were equipped with only rifles, carbines and machine guns; their orders were to retreat if there was opposition.

Britain and France consulted, and did nothing. Finally they, Belgium and Italy registered a protest. If there was ever a time for "bud-nipping" this was it. The League of Nations turned out to be a debating society, with no enforcing mechanism. The United States sat on the sidelines, witnessing Germany's aggression into Poland in 1939, Belgium and France and air attacks on Britain, until Japan, allied with Germany, attacked Pearl Harbor on December 7, 1941.

I don't want to get too far into it at this point, but it is interesting to conjecture as to whether an effective organization existing at the time, with on-call forces available, as well as with powers of embargo, sanctions and blockade, could not only have squelched the foray into the Rhineland but could also have prevented Hitler's massive buildup of military force; loosely analogous to what was done to Saddam Hussein in Iraq—his forces decimated, his country powerless. Certainly the history of Europe could have been considerably different .

James L Stokesbury, author of "Short History of World War II," opines that, "We now have sufficient evidence not only that Hitler could have been stopped, but the Western Powers knew he could have been stopped, had they the will to do it when it could have been done short of war.[1]"

I opine that under my assumption above he could have been stopped regardless.

Japan's Bud

The seeds of WWII in the Pacific were sown by Japan's invasion of Port Arthur in 1931 and then, using it as an excuse, invading Chinese-held territory in Manchuria. Japan's motivation was much the same as German Lebensraum, the professed need for living room. Japan's population was increasing by one million a year. Searching for a solution they turned to militarism. In February 1932 Japan announced the creation of a new state, Manchukuo. In 1936 it joined with Germany in the Anti-Communist Pact, creating "The Axis." The League of Nations chided Japan, whereupon it walked out of the League. In 1937 Japan began a full-scale invasion of China.

The rest is well known history. In a few short years it gobbled up much of China, the rim of Asia all the way to Burma, Malaysia, Singapore, Midway, the Philippines and many other islands. In October, 1941, General Tojo became Premier. Two months later Japan attacked Pearl Harbor.

It seems clear to me that the placing of a naval blockade between Japan and the mainland of Asia on the very first foray, thus bottling up Japan, could have nipped Japan's aggression in the bud. In a week or two an effective blockade would create a shortage of fuel, bringing industry to a halt, not to mention the Japanese battleships. A collection of US, British and French warships would certainly have been be up to the task.

Once again a lesson from the past. In my view "bud-nipping" could well have prevented the entire WW II in the Pacific, history would have been written vastly differently.

[1]From a "Short History of World War II" by James L. Stokesbury, Copyright 1980, by permission of William Morrow and Company, Inc.

More on "bud nipping" later.

American losses in WW I totaled 53, 513 battle deaths, 63,195 other deaths and 204,002 wounded. Altogether 4,743,826 served. The costs (in 1997 dollars), $508.9 billion. DOD. Opponents' battle deaths: 3,385,500.[2]

American losses in WW II totaled 292,131 battle deaths, 115,185 other deaths and 671, 846 wounded. Altogether 16,353,659 served. The costs (in 1997 dollars), $3.96 trillion. DOD. Opponents' battle deaths: 5,408,494.[2]

[2] The Center for Defense Information, Washington D.C., email address, owner-weekly@mail.cdi.org

15

Lessons Learned from our Three Police Actions this Century

It is my plan in this chapter to provide an overview of our three police actions, a brief reminder of what they were about—and for those younger folks, a brief introduction. My main purpose though, is to make an assessment of the degree of success achieved, in terms of original objective, efficiency and costs, a sort of batting average if you will, in baseball terms.

Behind the scenes in both the Korean and Vietnam wars was the Soviet Union, our temporary ally in World War II, and China. By the outbreak of the Korean War the old WW I powers had been swept away and replaced by the Soviet Union and the United States. The Soviets were pressing their hegemonic goals on many fronts around the world. Our containment policy was set in place.

Highlights of the Korean War

Russia had interests in Korea as far back as the early 1900's, bordering as it did on Korea. Near the end of World War II in the Pacific, with Japan the occupier, the United States took an interest in Korea, prompted in part by the Soviets sweeping eastward through Manchuria. In General Order No. 1, General MacArthur set American rules for Japan's surrender. One of its provisions was that the Russians were to occupy Korea down to the 38th parallel, the Americans' the south. Within days of the signing of the armistice aboard the battleship Missouri on September 2, 1945 the Russians and

Americans signed an agreement separating Korea at the 38th parallel, an arbitrary line across the middle of the country.

The bright skies of 1945 had become covered with dark clouds, showing red; by 1950 the world was again an unfriendly place.

There is evidence that in 1945-46, contrary to America's belief, South Korea was not a part of the Soviet expansion plan, although at the time Trieste, middle eastern oil fields, Philippines, Greece and Turkey were under siege. On the other hand, the Soviets were no doubt unaware of the United State's new determination to oppose Communist expansion (NSC-68). According to historian Max Hastings, author of "The Korean War," "Had the Russians had any inkling Washington's newfound determination to seek a battleground upon which to challenge Communist expansion, it is profoundly unlikely that Moscow would ever have allowed the North Korean's invasion of June 1950 to take place." He claims that "the Russians sanctioned the attack." At this time many thousands of Korean Communist veterans were returned to North Korea from China.

The Russians initially occupied North Korea while the United States occupied the South. But the Russians soon vacated, leaving it in the hands of Kim IL Sung. Both sides set in motion the training and equipping of their client forces, the Soviets providing heavy tanks, artillery and aircraft, political and military advisors. The United States was reluctant to provide heavy arms for lack of trust in the political leadership in the South as Syngman Rhee, elected President, had become a dictator, making the creation of the nation most difficult. The United States did begin the training of South Korean forces.

By January of 1949 the last of the United States occupation troops had left Korea, leaving 500 in the Korea Military Advisory Group.

By 1950 both President Truman and Secretary of State Acheson had given speeches which excluded Korea from the United States defense (containment) perimeter. Then, on June 25, 1950 the well equipped North Koreans burst across the 38th parallel.

The United Nations mandate for war was based on the General Assembly vote of June 27, 1950 calling for assistance to repel the attack against the South and to restore international peace and security—resulting in the United Nations Force.

The Republic of Korea forces were ill-prepared and equipped. Action was taken to move in and build a rather massive force to slow the onslaught. A United Nations force was created, initially of United States forces, a British Brigade and three Royal Air Force squadrons. The brilliant Inchon landing on the west coast near Seoul turned the tide; the enemy was driven back in just three months.

It was on October 24, 1950 that General MacArthur gave the fateful order for an all-out pursuit to the Yalu River bordering China, having assured President Truman personally just 10 days earlier on Wake Island, that neither the Chinese nor the Soviets would intervene. Within days the advancing troops ran into Chinese troops. On November 8, the CIA estimated that there were 30,000 to 40,000 Chinese troops in Korea, with 700,000 poised across the border in Manchuria. By the end of the year there were 400,000 troops supporting the small North Korean Army. By the end of the year United Nations forces were forced to the south of Seoul.

On December 25, 1950 the Chinese crossed the 38th parallel, and headed south. Seoul was taken on January 4th. By March 13 the Communists started to withdraw across all fronts. On the 15th, The Eighth army retook Seoul, once again crossing the 38th parallel.

President Truman and General MacArthur crossed swords over an ill-timed release of a policy statement which preempted the president. On December 29, 1950 General MacArthur received a new directive: defend in successive positions . . . inflicting such damage to hostile forces in Korea as is possible, subject to primary consideration of the safety of your troops. McArthur was relieved of his command on April 12.

The last two years of the war consisted of jockeying for position and spasmodic attacks, taking more thousands of lives.

By July 10, 1951 the opposing sides sat down at the negotiating table at Panmunjom, although the fighting continued until July 27, 1953 when the armistice was signed. A new line had been established on June 17, 1953. We have had troops there for more than four decades—today 37,000 troops are still there.

The United Nations, then about two years old, played a role for the first time in a major war scenario. In September, 1947, despite Russian objections, the United States referred the future of Korea to the United Nations. On November 14th, the United States proposed that the United Nations supervise election of the Korean government, followed by independence and the withdrawal of foreign forces. The American plan was adopted 46 to 0, with the eastern bloc abstaining. Syngman Rhee was elected President of the Republic of Korea. No election took place in North Korea.

In January, 1950 the Soviet Delegates walked out of the United Nations Security Council, held in its temporary quarters at Lake Success, NY, in protest against the seating of the Chinese Nationalists instead of the Communists. Consequently, on June 25 came the vote condemning the North Koreans for their attack of the South, and called for a withdrawal to the 38th parallel. The vote was 9-0 (today the Security Council has 15 members). Had the Soviets been present and used their veto, the result on the ground would have been the same, according to historian Max Hastings. I understand there is another theory, yet to be documented, as to why the Soviets absented themselves from the Security Council. Having anticipated the aggression, the Soviets would have avoided a veto of the actions taken by its allies.

Their strategy: turn the fighting over to their proxies, the Chinese and the North Koreans; their own costs included just the materiel and training, their objective: to wear down the United States at no cost in Soviet lives. (There is room for this same conclusion in the Vietnam War: materiel and training, but no Soviet lives.)

The United Nations Force was made up initially of the American forces plus those of fifteen other nations, the largest being a British Commonwealth Division and three Air Force Squadrons. My assessment of the ratio of United States forces to other allies was about 95% of the total, what Robert McNamara referred to later in Vietnam, as the cosmetic treatment.[1]

The costs of the Korean war: 36,914 American were killed, with 103,284 wounded, 8177 missing or prisoners, a total of 5,764,143 Americans served in Korea. The estimated cost of the war to the US: $352 billion (in 1997 dollars). Opponent deaths, 500,000, wounded 1,000,000.[1]

Where was I in this period? I arrived at the Joint War Plans Office in the Air Staff, Pentagon before the truce was signed. My role

[1]Drawn from "The Korean War" by Max Hastings, a Touchstone Book, Simon and Schuster.

consisted in part of preparing positions papers for the Air Force Chief in his role as a member of the JCS on how to end the war. Needless to say none of the ideas proposed had any effect. The truce was signed, but an armistice has not yet been agreed as of this writing—37,000 US troops remain there after all these years.

I think it useful to have rating system for our major police actions this century for a number of reasons, the immediate one to help avoid pitfalls in planning future actions. For want of a better scoreboard on the conduct of the wars I've selected 10 as the optimum. So the following factors can only reduce the score. Before continuing, we all understand that hindsight is always 20-20.

The United States probably erred in sending mixed signals to the Communists as to its interest in Korea in the early 1950s. Also, in error, was the decision to pursue North Korean and Chinese forces north of the 38th parallel, the line agreed by the United States and the Soviets just after the armistice at the end of WW II. And it was a mistake fostering Syngman Rhee, who was not an optimum selection as the leader of South Korea. The lack of confidence among key officials in the highest echelons of our government certainly didn't foster sober judgments; and lastly, one could have wished for an armistice years ago so that our forces, still 37,000 strong, could have been redeployed—a costly forty-odd years. One could have wished, also, that it could have been a truly multilateral effort. Why did the United States carry the lion's share of the load during the war, and then the entire load in the ensuing years—while many other nations have reaped the benefit?

Nothing of what I've said in any way detracts from the performance of our troops in the war there; in my view, in the situation into which they were thrust and with the arms they were provided they performed, and still perform, in typical Yankee (we are all Yankees to others) style. And, of course, the support the United States has given South Korea since the war has been a major factor in its economic success.We enjoy the automobiles and TVs produced there. All of us familiar with the current disparity between the North and the South today, actually a famine is taking place in the North at the moment.

My score for the Korean War : 8

Highlights of the Vietnam War

The Vietnam War will be dealt with briefly, as described at the beginning of this chapter.

Recall that Japan occupied Indochina (henceforth called Vietnam) during WW II. After the occupation Ho Chi Minh (the same one who proposed independence for Vietnam to President Wilson incident to the Treaty of Versailles) announced the independence of Vietnam. After WWII the United States acquiesced to France's return to Vietnam. As in Korea, a line was drawn across Vietnam, separating the North from the South. The United States supported the French; China and the Soviet Union supported Ho Chi Minh. In 1954, after the defeat of the French at Dien Bien Phu, the United States assumed responsibility from France for the protection of Vietnam, south of the partition line running east and west near the center of Vietnam. At the same time the United States had negotiated a treaty, the Southeast Asia Treaty Organization (SEATO), designed in part to protect Vietnam. I was the United States representative at the first meeting of the Military Staff Planners of SEATO, in Hawaii. SEATO withered on the vine.

It was later that I wrote the message that started the flow of what eventually would become more than 543,000 troops being sent to Vietnam (altogether 8,744,000 served there). All in all I was involved with Vietnam for about eight years, before and during the war, as discussed earlier. There is little to be learned by a lengthy rehash of the war. The United States tried every stratagem, massive carpet bombing by B-52s, mining waterways (being careful to avoid waterways frequented by Soviet supply ships—which freely came and went to Hanoi all through the war), destroying air defenses (all provided by the Soviets), even employing night vision-equipped airplanes—called gunships—for attacking truck convoys at night on jungle roads, defoliating trees to expose the enemy (the toxicity of Agent Orange is still a matter of controversy), beefing up the political leadership in Saigon—all to save South Vietnam. Over a half-million American troops did not turn the tide. What we will never know is whether massive bombing from the start would have made a difference. (In order that I could say after the war that I was engaged in combat—unlike my combat experience in WW II—I arranged to ride on a B-52 as a high ranking crew member—without any duties on a carpet bombing mission to the Demilitarized Military Zone, having taken off from Guam, air-refueled over the Philippines and returning to Guam).

The ebb and flow of the war continued for eleven years. The fact is that the United States introduced combat forces into Vietnam in 1964 and walked out in 1975, leaving the South Vietnamese to fend for themselves. i.e., to be swallowed up by North Vietnam.

Recall that at the time of the Tonkin Gulf affair I was working in the Pacific Division, Operations in the Joint Staff, the Pentagon at the time the JCS were to make a recommendation to Secretary McNamara and the President as to massive force deployments to Vietnam. I broke the rules by walking up to the 4th floor to the Air Staff to talk with a senior staffer whom I knew had the ear of the Air Force Chief. I urged that he relate my views and that he vote "no" as to the deployments. I had that solid inner feeling that our troops would be fighting in jungle terrain which favored the North Vietnamese troops, making our sophisticated weapons far less effective, and that we would become mired down as were the French. Also, I thought that in principle sending massive troops to fight on the mainland of Asia was a mistake. Obviously, those much my senior did not share those views—even after the experience of Korea. After that day, I never raised the matter again during the war—even when my WW II friends were railing me about its conduct. Many did not understand that for a military man, in uniform or out, when the President makes a decision, like it or not, it is to be carried out. Without that loyalty and discipline, a military force would not be worthy of the name. (Years later my WW II friends and I have carried on sober conversations).

When I first heard about former Secretary of Defense Robert McNamara's book on Vietnam, "In Retrospect," I thought that he was opening the wounds of those who served in Vietnam, that the book would be a disservice and that waiting thirty-odd years to admit mistakes was too much and too long.

Having read McNamara's book only recently, I now admire him for his fortitude and consider his conclusions and recommendations a valuable service to our nation. Profiting by our mistakes and

shortcomings is what this book is about, too. He does a superb job
of analyzing the shortcomings of our government with respect to the
War. Ten of his "eleven major causes for disaster in Vietnam," shown
below with his permission, are a great service to our nation. I am in
full agreement with them all. Several could be applied to the Korean
War and you will recognize that many apply equally to today. Several of his eleven points will be discussed again in Chapter 6 in re-
lation to the Quadrennial Defense Review. His eleventh point (not
shown here) will be discussed later.

"1. We misjudged then—as we have since—the geopolitical intentions of our adversaries (in this case, North Vietnam and the Vietcong, supported by China and the Soviet Union), and we exaggerated
the dangers to the United States of their actions

2. We viewed the people and their leaders of South Vietnam in
terms of our own existence. We saw in them a thirst for—and a determination to fight for—freedom and democracy. We totally misjudged
the political forces within the country.

3. We misunderstood the power of nationalism to motivate a
people (in this case, the North Vietnamese and the Vietcong) to fight
and die for their beliefs and values—and we continue to do so in many
parts of the world.

4. Our misjudgments of friends and foe alike reflected our profound ignorance of the history, culture, and politics of the people in the
area, and the personalities and habits of their leaders. We might have
made similar misjudgments regarding the Soviets during our frequent
confrontations—over Berlin, Cuba, the Middle East, for example—
had we not had the advice of Tommy Thompson, Chip Bolen, and
George Kennan. These senior diplomats had spent decades studying
the Soviet Union, its people and its leaders, why they behaved as they
did, and how they would react to our actions. Their advice proved invaluable in shaping our judgments and decision. No Southeast Asia
counterparts existed for senior officials to consult when making decisions on Vietnam.

5. We failed then—as we have since—to recognize the limitations of modern, high-technology military equipment, forces, and doctrine in confronting unconventional, highly motivated people's
movements. We failed as well to adapt our military tactics to the task of
winning the hearts and minds of people from a totally different culture.

6. We failed to draw Congress and the American people onto a full and frank discussion of the pros and cons of a large-scale US military involvement in Southeast Asia before we initiated action.

7. After the action got under way and unanticipated events forced us off our planned course, we failed to retain popular support in part because we did not explain fully what was happening and why we were doing what we did. We had not prepared the public to understand the complex events we faced and how to react constructively to the need for changes in course as the nation confronted uncharted seas and an alien environment, A nation's deepest strength lies not in its military prowess but, rather, in the unity of its people. We failed to maintain it.

8. We did not recognize that neither our people nor our leaders are omniscient. Where our own security is not directly at stake, our judgment of what is in another people's or country's interest should be put to the test of open discussion in international forums. We do not have the God-given right to shape every nation in our own image or as we chose.

9. We did not hold to the principle that US military action—other than in response to direct threats to our own security—should be carried out only in conjunction with multinational forces supported fully (and not merely cosmetically) by the international community.

10. We failed to recognize that in international affairs, as in other aspects of life, there may be problems for which there are no immediate solutions. For one whose life has been dedicated to the belief and practice of problem solving, this is particularly hard to admit. But, at times, we may have to live with an imperfect, untidy world."[2]

Participation by the United Nations was non-existent.

Casualties: United States: 58,177 Americans were killed in combat, 153,303 wounded. Altogether 8,744,000 troops served in Vietnam. The cost: $755.3 billion (in 1997 dollars). Allied Casualties: 5225. Army of Vietnam casualties: 211,480. Center for Defense Information, Washington, DC. 1997 CDI Military Almanac.

[2]"In Retrospect" by Robert McNamara, Copyright Times Books, Random House, Inc., 201 East 50th Street, NY, NY 10022

SVN opponents' deaths 1,130,038, 1,000,000 SVN civilian casualties, 6,5000,000 war refugees.[3]

My score on the Vietnam War : 0

Again, our servicemen did their duty. Their leaders let them down.

Korea-Vietnam Wrap Up

The master plan for the Soviets would have had as its aim the weakening of the United States by seducing it into combat halfway around the world, weakening its fiscal soundness, depleting its resources and taking as many American lives as possible. The Russians were a canny, crafty lot, until Gorbachev. The leaders of a country that would kill millions of its own—including the Czar's family—to attain and maintain power would not think twice about manipulating its client states to sacrifice the lives of their people to satisfy its quest for hegemony.

With that as their objective the Soviets succeeded handily, first, in terms of the lives cost to the Russians—0, the United States— 406,601 dead and wounded. It was the US and allies fighting the tentacles of an octopus—a Russian octopus with Chinese gloves. They provided materiel: tanks, artillery, aircraft and supplies in both wars plus a sophisticated air defense system with ground-to-air missiles in the case of Vietnam. The United States did the same, but had to ship it and the troops halfway around the world.

At the end, the Soviets had one and one-half nations in their orbit to show for their efforts. As destiny would have it, though, some thirty years later, under the leadership of Gorbachev and Yeltsin the Soviet Union no longer exists. In fairness, though, in the overall final analysis it was the perseverance of the United States on all fronts that had much to do with the collapse of Soviet Communism. The

[3] Reprinted with permission from The World Almanac and Book of Facts 1997, Copyright 1997 PRIMEDIA Reference, Inc. All rights reserved.

other side of that coin, however, was the recognition by the Soviets that their touted economic system simply did not work; they were forced to change it, throwing in a democratic system to boot.

The unified Vietnam, too, has moved toward a market economy, courting foreign automobile assembly plants. The United States has opened a diplomatic office there. Kim IL Sung in North Korea holds on to the old Communist mantle—his people starving. The Republic of Korea is a showplace by comparison.

The cost of both wars: 348, 403 Americans killed and wounded and $1.131 trillion (in 1997 dollars). Center for Defense Information, Washington DC).

The scoreboard at this point: 4

I think this quotation is most apt at this point—

"There are two things which will always be very difficult for a democratic nation : to start a war and to end it."[4]

Highlights of the Gulf War

The Gulf War (Desert Storm) was a war of a wholly different character. Saddam Hussein sent his forces across a national border into Kuwait. First, a key difference was the terrain. Instead of the mountainous terrain of Korea and the jungles of Vietnam, in Iraq the land is fairly flat, at least in the south, much of it traversable by wheeled vehicles; the dry air provides good visibility most of the time. Another key difference, though, was the fact that the United Nations Security Council was in charge throughout.

The Gulf War was a textbook peacemaking police action in many ways. President Bush early on obtained the support of Congress,

[4] From De Tocqueville's "Democracy in Action."

contrary to the initiation of the Korean War. In addressing Congress he said, "The crisis in the Persian Gulf, as grave as it is, also offers a rare opportunity to move toward an historic period of cooperation . . . a new world order can emerge: a new era, free from threat of terror, stronger in the pursuit of justice, and more secure in the quest for peace." His was a noteworthy breakthrough, laying the war in the lap of the United Nations Security Council. In all, the Security Council issued eleven resolutions in the first week, putting Saddam Hussein on a short rein. Russia supported them all.

Within hours the air battle was virtually over, air superiority attained. In six months the entire affair was over. At war's end the Iraqi's had lost 86% of their tanks, 64% of armored personnel carriers and 69% of their artillery. There is no question that the air campaign was a stunning success, but only recently have Defense Department claims been refuted. The General Accounting Office reported that, for example, the F-117, the Stealth Fighter, hit 80% of it targets during the war; the GAO then reported that "the percentage might be as low a 40%." Another, the F-15E Fighter, claimed by it manufacturer to be "all weather," which the GAO said its "ability to detect and identify targets through clouds, smoke and dust was very limited." The report indicated that "there had been a pattern of overstatement by the Pentagon." Take note that Saddam Hussein was not deterred by our stockpile of nuclear weapons.

I imagine few people know that the US was reimbursed for taking the lead in the fighting, for supplying the preponderance of the troops. Early on a formula was established whereby participating nations and Japan and Germany would pay the US, making it a mercenary or, to be blunt, a "hired gun." If this is to be the pattern for the future, God help us. Any "blood money" should be paid to the United Nations general fund, removing any incentive for the US to repeat this formula. The conduct of this war is another demonstration of the need to do combined preplanning, to include a fair share of forces from all interested nations. Japan and Germany should reevaluate their prohibition of deploying troops when engaged in Security Council authorized operations.[5]

[5] Based on "The Gulf Conflict" by Freedman and Karsh, Princeton University Press

It is noteworthy that only 148 Americans died in combat—in contrast to the casualties in the other two police actions. Other coalition members killed: 92, with total combined casualties of 1016. Coalition deaths 92, opponents deaths 40,000. Troops deployed: American, 467, 539; coalition total, 795,000.

The cost to the US: $7.6 billion ; as other nations reimbursed the US $53.7 billion (in 1997 dollars). DOD.

Opponent deaths by the Center for Defense Information, Washington, D.C.

The scoreboard for the Gulf War : 8.5 (No deduction was made for the Defense Department's overstated claims).

The combined scoreboard for all three Police Actions : 5. 5

How does one interpret this scoreboard number? In the simplest of terms I see it as a measure of effectiveness—the original mission vs. the result—on average, slightly more than half of the optimum. Were the three police actions worth the cost in lives and treasure? We're now at status quo ante, much as where we started in Korea, out of Vietnam and have for now only a small flow of oil from Iraq (due to the embargo as a lesson to Saddam Hussein, the small amount allowed by the Security Council for food and medicine), no doubt raising world oil prices slightly. Looking at it another way, how would our national security have been affected had we not engaged militarily in any of these cases? I realize that revisionism is highly arguable, but I submit that in the case of the Far East it would be much the same as it is today. The Communist system was flawed from the beginning—which was finally recognized by its leaders. I argue, in the case of Iraq, that acting as the world's "hired gun" is not the way to go (which does not mean that his aggression should not have been stopped. Another way could or should have been available. More on this later).

So the next logical question is when should the US intercede militarily in strength? There will be much more on this in upcoming chapters.

Iraq ll

Here is where I stopped writing the chapter, but on January 13, 1998 Saddam Hussein, kicking off his traces, refused to allow UNSCOM and IAEA inspectors into site—including his touted palaces—suspected of harboring or making weapons of mass destruction; too, he accused a US member of the multi-national inspection team of spying for America. His action, a violation of the terms of the UN Security Council Resolution 687 of 1991, to which Saddam had agreed; in short, he simply thumbed his nose at the Security Council.

For an uneasy and uncertain six weeks the airwaves carried the differing views of a number of nations. Only two nations, the US and the United Kingdom agreed to bombing Iraq. Others, including Russia, France and China, all Permanent Members of the Security Council, and Iran, Iraq, Kuwait, Saudi Arabia and others—and key members of our own congress—were not unified as to an appropriate response. Russia opposed the use of force. It developed that Russia, France and Iran have commercial interests in assisting Iraq to restore its oil drilling and pumping capabilities. In any event the US early on ordered the fleet and other forces to the Persian Gulf area.

Moving now to the bottom line, I see the outcome as a boon to the Security Council and a coup by Kofi Annan, UN Secretary-General. Amidst all the chatter and clutter between nations over several weeks, Saddam Hussein is back where he was, warned by a Security Council Resolution that "any violation would have the severest consequences for Iraq." To me the basic strategy employed was so smooth it could well have been orchestrated from the beginning. It was as though Kofi Annan and Bill Clinton had a huddle— or even a phone conversation—early on. By the end of the conversation a simple strategy had been developed as follows: Bill's role: move forces forward, with much fanfare and ancillary "town meetings" to heighten the suspense, to inform the American people, but principally, by deploying forces to pressure Saddam Hussein to back down. Kofi's role: at the strategic moment obtain a date with Saddam to negotiate an agreement to return to the status quo ante.

There is some credence for this theory. Romesh Ratnesar reported in a Time article, March , 1998, "A Star Turn for the Peace Broker," that "Last week he [Kofi Annan] praised the US show of strength in the Gulf, saying 'The best way to use force is to show force in order not to use it. . . . But while Annan respects American power he is not captive to it.'" In meetings with President Clinton and Secretary of State Albright, Annan makes his bottom line clear by asserting, "This is very important to me . . . that if the US had gone ahead, it would have divided not only the UN but the international community . . . a good leader must be a good follower."[6] Of course that kind of talk drives congressional conservatives batty. (Had the US gone ahead on it own, by my reading the US would have been in violation of the UN Charter. More on this later.)

Under this strategy not a single life was lost, the fifteen nations at the Security Council OK'd the Resolution unanimously. The many nations that were squabbling over every facet of the matter were placated—for the time being.

The handling of this affair not only puts a feather in Kofi's hat for his handling of the matter but moves the UN and the Security Council a few light years closer to its original purpose—to secure peace and security. It demonstrated the "possible." During the posturing phase only two nations saw eye-to-eye, the US and Great Britain, the many other vocal nations had their own axes to grind. The process of attaining international law—which this was—was anything but tidy, but to me, represents the hope of the future.

Having passed out some plaudits though, there are a number of important lessons to be learned which require deliberation and action. The IRAQ II episode presents such great lessons that now, as the dust is settling, is the time to take advantage of them—to explore solutions.

A New American Mini-Strategy for Iraq

Some assumptions for a different scenario:

One, that the Security Council has an in-being Charter-authorized Peace Force, with a capability to project military power anywhere on the globe in a reasonably short time.

[6] "A Star Turn for the Peace Broker." By Romesh Ratensar, Time. March 3, 1998.

Two, that the Security Council has its authorized full, experienced military staff, adequate for war planning. And that Saddam Hussein is well aware that the Security Council's new Combined Military Staff already has a plan in hand to deal with Iraq's anticipated violations with military action.

Three, that the International Criminal Court has been established, has indicted Saddam Hussein for his many war crimes, and is, in fact, trying him in absentia.

Under this new Mini-Strategy Saddam is not likely in similar straits to again thumb his nose at the Security Council and to the world. Let's assume he is even more of a megalomaniac than had been thought; here's a new script for his January 13, 1998 act: Saddam Hussein prohibits the UNSCOM inspectors from entering the sites suspected of making or storing biological , chemical or nuclear weapons. The next day the US Ambassador to the UN presents a draft resolution to the Security Council, to wit, permit UNSCOM inspectors to proceed immediately, or that "violation would have severest consequences." No fanfare, no fuss, just implementing international law.

Under this Mini-Strategy one would expect the same unanimous vote by the Security Council as in the actual situation.

This scenario could be a model for dealing with all rogue nations. More on this. (Actually, it's the heads of nations that are the rogues, but for lack of a better term I'll continue to use the term "rogue nations.")

In an introspective article by Fred M. Ikle, former Undersecretary of Defense, says "But much of today's thinking on international arms control is totally unreasonable—especially the legalistic American approach that dominates world diplomacy. . . . That no violation goes punished under international arms-control regimes is a lesson Saddam has patiently tried to teach us for a long time." He then recites that "In the early 1980's he used chemical weapons in a war that he started against Iran . . . [which] violated one of the oldest arms-control treaties, to which Iraq was also a party, the Geneva Protocol of 1925, which even Hitler did not violate." Ikle goes on, "The world had not learned the lesson, so the great teacher Saddam patiently tried again. He used poison gas to rub human rights violations into skin and eyes of Iraq's own people. . . . The great teacher thought this would make it plain that the real problem was not lack of verification but a total lack of penalties once violations are detected. To no avail. The world community chose not to learn the lesson."

Then, Saddam "kept asserting that Iraq no longer had any prohibited weapons until, one day, his son-in-law defected and began revealing facts to the contrary. Then . . . he admitted he had lied, he let the United Nations inspectors destroy some of his chemical weapons (having sworn before that he had kept none)—and he suffered no penalty. [He also slaughtered a number of his own family who defected]. Saddam again tried to teach this lesson. During the past few months he has demonstrated that international weapons inspectors can be denied all access for a long period of time and then—as a gesture of peacefulness—be readmitted in exchange for a big reward . . . the lifting of the oil embargo."

Lastly, he warned that "Anyone with any experience in these areas [international inspection] has to admit that biological weapons can be so easily concealed that a dictatorship intent on hiding them cannot be found out. However, the international verification system will not only be incapable of catching determined violators, it will also tutor the participating officials from rogue nations in how better to conceal their violations and, as part of their international tour of duty, let them in on the latest ideas for making more lethal biological weapons."[7]

Thank you, Saddam Hussein, for imparting to us no end of lessons. It is cause for deep sadness that we are in incapable of learning what you so diligently taught us. I trust UNSCOM is screening its inspectors to close that loophole. Thankfully, weapons other than chemical and biological cannot be easily concealed.

In early 1998 Secretary of Defense Cohen announced that 25 nations have or are developing doomsday weapons. A DOD report showed that just in the Mideast, Iran, Iraq, Syria, Israel, Egypt and

---

[7] Fred M. Ikle's "Saddam's Lessons in Arms Control," Wall Street Journal, March 4, 1998. Republication by permission of Dow Jones, Inc. via Copyright Clearance Center, Inc. (C) 1998, Dow Jones and Company, Inc. All rights reserved.

Libya, all have either or both chemical and biological weapon capability, four are developing or have a nuclear weapon capability and all six have or are working on advanced missile technology. What Secretary Cohen did not announce was a solution.

Neil King, Jr. sums up the situation. "Relatively cheap and easy to obtain, biological weapons have become the world's great equalizers. The US may have stealth fighter jets and laser-guided cruise missiles, but give a weak country a few rockets armed with anthrax and the world's last superpower can't help but take notice." He quotes Secretary of Defense Cohen as saying "Such weapons give 'disproportionate power' to 'regional aggressors, third-rate armies, terrorist cells and even religious cults.'" King went on, "Baghdad upped the ante as it rushed to develop long-range missile technology by combining Soviet-supplied Scud missiles with technology and expertise from countries like China, Germany, Austria and Italy according to official reports. . . . " and that "Iraq was prepared to launch hundreds of missiles[in 1991] armed with biological agents, against Israel and Western troops if the regime itself were put under threat."

"Iran moved quickly in the mid-1980s to amass stockpiles of mustard gas and cyanide weapons, which it used against Iraq toward the end of the war. Syria developed at least one major nerve-gas production center, while in North Africa, Libya pushed for self-sufficiency opening its own chemical-weapons facility in 1988, thanks mostly to European technology."

"Much of the spread springs from basic economics. With the Soviet Union no longer around to provide cheap arms and ready financing, defense spending on conventional arms has plunged across the Muslim world. Libya spends less than $50 million a year on imported arms, down from a high of $2. 8 billion, says a report by the Washington-based Center for Strategic and International Studies. . . . As one arms specialist puts it, 'Nerve gas and anthrax are filling in for a lack of tanks.'"[8] Another reason to implement the Mini-Strategy for America!

[8] Neil King's article, "Iraq Is One of Many With a Doomsday Arsenal," Wall Street Journal, February, 1998. Republication by permission of Dow Jones, Inc. via Copyright Clearance Center, Inc. (C) 1998, Dow Jones and Company, Inc. All rights reserved.

Today, the US pays the lion share of the bill. Why is it that the US has taken upon itself to provide the overwhelming majority of forces in this affair, to be world policemen and, as you will discover later, in many more situations?

At the end of Iraq ll Senator Warner called attention to the fact that the US had run up a bill of $750,000 above ordinary operating expenses simply by deploying the forces to the Persian Gulf and indicated that costs would continue to increase so long as the forces remain. Conversely, Saddam Hussein's costs were virtually nil. Wily, eh? Shrewd as he is, triggering these costs may have been a part of his game plan.

Sen. Ted Stevens (R-Alaska), the committee chairman said, "Our nation bears a unique burden, as sole remaining global military superpower. But the capability does not imply we must go it alone in every crisis, in every emergency."

A few days later the administration submitted a request to congress for $1.36 billion which would be to sustain the build-up of US forces in the Persian Gulf to come on top of the $677.5 million budgeted for normal US military operations in the gulf region in the fiscal year ending September 30.

In succeeding chapters the issues about the role of the US as world policeman will be addressed, its deployment and employment of forces unilaterally, in situations of community interest, and the matter of financing.

Thank you, Saddam, for teaching us how to deal with leaders such as you.

16

The White House and the Department of Defense (DOD) on National Security Strategy

President Clinton signed a cardinal document, "A National Security Strategy for the New Century," in May 1997; that same month the Department of Defense (DOD) issued a supporting document, "The Quadrennial Defense Review" (QDR).

The President's Policy

First, a look at the President's twenty-nine page paper. It is in a matter of speaking a masterfully written, comprehensive document detailing the programs for enhancing US security. It points to the threats to US interests and the need for integrated approaches, diplomacy, international assistance, arms control, nonproliferation initiatives and military activities. It seems to cover all the bases. Under the heading of "Shaping the International Environment, the United States has a range of tools at its disposal with which to shape the international environment in ways favorable to US interests and global security." And later . . . "Through Military Activities . . . The US military plays an essential role in building coalitions and shaping the international environment in ways that protect and promote US interests." (Underlining provided).

At the outset I want to be on record as saying that I am just as interested in protecting and promoting US vital interests as is the

President of the United States; I spent more than thirty years working actively to enhance them.

These policy statements seem straightforward enough but what
happens if, for example, China announces a new national security
strategy stating, "China has a range of tools available at its disposal
to shape the international environment in ways favorable to Chinese
interests and global security" . . . and "The Chinese military plays an
essential role in building coalitions and shaping the international
environment in ways that protect and promote China's interests." Or
that Russia announces the same new policy. To carry it to the point
of absurdity, that many other nations announce the same policy.

Doesn't the announcement of such a policy set up confrontational situations? Isn't it simply a continuation of a nation seeking
advantage over others? The US, superpower, the only nation that
can project military power most anywhere in the world, has become
the world's super policeman (self-appointed), but these capabilities
are enlarged now by assuming the role of judge, too—also self-
appointed. In fact, as the President's document is of keen interest to
virtually all nations, many must be wondering how the United States
intends to shape them. Their senior officials must have this thought
in mind when meeting with US officials. And conceivably, they may
come to the conclusion that meeting under the stated ground rules
would be a waste of time, having to play on a such a tilted playing
field. Who wants to hear a lecture?

Being the superpower with global reach is like having an itch—
one can't keep his hands quiet.

To avoid even the appearance of the "us" vs." them" pattern, a
restated President's policy could well be:

> The United States will use its power and influence to institute and
> perfect international Rule of Law through international institutions.
> It's primary objective is that of preventing aggression and other viola-
> tions of international law. It's military forces and activities will be pre-
> pared to join others in enforcing international law consistent with its
> Constitution and in accord with negotiated agreements.
>
> The United States is ready and willing to not only discuss any na-
> tional security or other matter with any nation at any time, but to come to
> terms, to reach genuine accommodation, and to assist in any feasible way.

The current President's policy reflects a bygone era when there were, indeed, enemies. The Soviet Union is the only nation which has the capacity to inflict mortal damage to the US. Today, however, there are no enemies seriously threatening US national security, which does not mean that serious potential threats may not arise. Now is the moment to shift gears after several million years in the jungle, to start afresh with Rule of Law.

An interesting question. How different would the President's policy statement be if the US were not the world superpower? It certainly would be considerably different. And why shouldn't the policy be the same in any event? In the larger sense, virtually all nations strive for the same things: uninterrupted commerce, security, prosperity, health, etc. The only conclusion one can come to is that the present US policy is based on force and, yes, intimidation. In the long term the only way to promote US interests is in cooperation with others. And it is axiomatic that to have security there must be peace. The above restatement of US policy would fill the bill.

The United States has the finest institutions yet devised, so great that many nations have emulated those of the United States, and for which others aspire. Yes, we are a great nation, great enough to allow others to shape their own destinies in peaceful ways. As many nations look to the United States as the leader of the Free World it is obligated to set an example, even promote dialogue with those nations we admire the least. (Recall, I was a part of citizen dialogue with the enemy during the Cold War—in the Soviet Union—on three occasions. Likewise, citizen diplomacy between Americans and others with such nations a Iran, Iraq, Syria, Libya, North Korea and others would be useful now. Overtures were started with Iran only recently).

None should infer from the above that the US shouldn't maintain an adequate, first class military.

I leave this restatement of policy hanging in midair until later, when bridges have been crossed; then we'll revisit it.

An interesting postscript. I searched the twenty-nine pages of the President's document to find any reference to the United Nations, finding only one: "The contemporary era was forged by steadfast American leadership over the last half century—through efforts such as the Marshall Plan, NATO, the United Nations and the World Bank." Yes, all fine institutions, but the irony is that the US is not fully using the institution which the US had a leading role in forging, the UN. It hasn't really begun to take advantage of the UN's potential after more that fifty years—for lack of US leadership. Nor did I detect any reference to the United Nations in the Defense QDR, the bible for military policy to the year 2015. Simply put, the US for the most part, has a blind eye for the Security Council (More on this later).

And Now the Department of Defense Quadrennial Review (QDR)

I wish there were a simpler way of examining the QDR. It does become rather technical, but bear with me.

As of May 1997, the new sixty-nine page QDR is published at the direction of Congress. It reflects and expands on the White House document. It's most important. Its stated purpose, to examine:

> "America's defense needs from 1997 to 2015: potential threats, strategy, force structure, readiness posture, military modernization programs, defense infrastructure, and other elements of the defense program. The QDR is intended to provide a blueprint for a strategy-based, balanced, and affordable defense program."

The QDR, also, has been masterfully crafted. A summary of the QDR is not only appropriate but essential to get the essence of where the Defense Department (DOD) plans to take us in strategic terms. An effort has been made to select representative passages.

Secretary of Defense Cohen appears to have taken full charge of the Department of Defense. He uses quite accurately this phrase in his cover letter of the QDR, ". . . we developed an overarching *defense strategy* to deal with the world today and tomorrow." The report states, "The United States is the only superpower to deal with the world today and tomorrow, and it is expected to remain so throughout the 1997-2015 period."

As will be shown later, it is of considerable significance that the State Department does not issue a counterpart to the Defense QDR, leaving a void, and resulting in an uncoordinated national policy.

As to US national security strategy the QDR opts between two views: "focus our . . . energies at home and only committing military forces where our survival is at stake" and, alternatively "the world's only remaining superpower . . ." which is "generally protecting peace and stability around the globe." Between these two is: "A strategy of engagement . . . presumes the United States will continue to exercise strong leadership in the international security environment . . . ensuring peace and stability in the regions where the United States has a vital interest."

The QDR speaks of "the capability to act unilaterally" while "the challenges we face demands cooperative, multinational-national approaches that distributes the burdens of responsibility among like-minded states." Then, "We are the only power in the world that can organize effective military responses to large-scale regional threats."

Under the heading Shaping the International Environment, the QDR repeats the President's statements, "The Department of Defense has an essential role to play in shaping the international security environment in ways favorable to US interests." And ". . . through Military Activities . . . The military plays an essential role in building coalitions and shaping the international environment in ways that promote and protect US interests." (Underlining supplied).

America's Vital Interests

A key section, again reflecting the President's document, is quoted intact: "Nevertheless, both US national interests and limited resources argue for the *selective* use of US forces. The primary purpose is to deter and defeat the threat of organized violence against the United States and it interests. Decisions about whether and when to use military forces should be guided, first and foremost, by the national interest at stake—be they vital, important, or humanitarian in nature—and by whether the costs and risks of a particular military involvement are commensurate with those interests. When the interests at stake are vital—that is, they are of broad, overriding importance to the survival, security, and vitality of the United States—we should do whatever it takes to defend them, including, <u>when necessary, the unilateral use of military power.</u> US vital interests include, but are not limited to:

> QDR 1 * "Protecting the sovereignty, territory, and population of the United States, and preventing and deterring threats to our homeland, including NBC (Nuclear, Biological and Chemical) attacks and terrorism;
>
> QDR 2 * Preventing emergence of a hostile regime, regional coalition or hegemon;
>
> QDR 3 * Ensuring freedom of the seas and security of international sea lines of communication, airways and space;
>
> QDR 4 * Ensuring uninhibited access to key markets, energy supplies, and strategic resources;
>
> QDR 5 * Deterring and, if necessary, defeating aggression against US ,allies and friends."
>
> (Underlining supplied).

What Does International Law Say?

The above military actions vary widely in both scope and timing. A missile attack on the US could demand an instant reply, for example. Likewise, an incident at sea could require immediate action. I note that these situations are provided for in Art. 51 of the UN Charter which states that: "Nothing . . . shall impair the inherent right of individual or collective self-defense if an armed attack occurs against a Member of the United Nations until the Security Council has taken measures necessary to maintain international peace and security. Measures taken by members in the exercise of this right of self-defense shall be immediately reported to the Security Council and shall not in any way affect the authority and responsibility of the Security Council to take at any time such actions as it deems necessary in order to maintain or restore international peace and security." Self-defense is thus a limited emergency measure that is permissible only if there is an armed attack against a UN Member and only until the Security Council can act.

All other actions outlined would occur over time when rationality can be employed, allowing for the implementation of existing unilateral or combined war plans or for the preparation of new plans. In these cases *the Security Council calls the shots.* Article 24 of the UN Charter provides that "In order to ensure prompt and effective action by the United Nations, its members confer on the Security Council primary responsibility for the maintenance of international peace and security, and agree that in carrying out its duties under this responsibility the Security Council acts in their behalf." Article 39 states, "The Security Council shall determine the existence of any threat to the peace, breach of the peace or act of aggression, and shall make recommendations, or decide what measures shall be taken in accordance with Articles 41 and 42, to maintain or restore international peace and security." Recall that Article 41 states that "The Security Council may decide what measures not involving the use of armed forces are to be employed . . ." and in Article 42 that "Should *the Security Council* consider that measures provided for in Article 41 would be inadequate or have proved to be inadequate, it may take such actions by air, sea or land forces as may be necessary to maintain or restore international peace and security." (Underlining supplied).

Do you detect a dichotomy here? Do you get the same reaction to the QDR as I do, that there appears to be a cavalier disregard for international law? Certainly the US would take any matter that involved its vital interests to the Security Council. Because by my reading, should it not do so it would not only be the world policeman, but a rogue world policeman. I am astounded that the QDR does not even mention the United Nations or the Security Council in any of its sixty-nine pages. Virtually nothing is said as to how the US will operate within international law, or even that it intends to. Note that Security Council Resolutions constitute international law.

Does it seem that the Department of Defense and the Security Council are on different planets? How many times is it stated in the QDR that "the US will act unilaterally if necessary," implying that our allies either cannot act for lack of forces or do not agree with the US position on a matter involving international law or other reasons? After all, why should they risk their forces? Let the US do it. By the wording of the QDR like-minded nations can rest on their oars, spend their money on whatever else they may choose.

I'm most curious about the State Department position on the "unilateral actions" which involve international law, as examples of the sea lanes and airways. It is rather obvious that the State Department had little voice in the preparation of the QDR. In this connection it just happened that I attended a briefing in 1993 in the Pentagon by an Assistant Secretary of Defense on the then new Bottom Up Review. My questions was, "Has the Defense Department coordinated with State?" He did not answer the question. I cannot imagine that the president has approved in advance unilateral action in such situations.

Granted, the DOD takes its orders from our Commander in Chief, the political head of our nation, who makes the final decision on every use of the armed forces (and the Congress needs to provide the funds) and who cannot ignore the fact that in his role as President he is obligated to raise in the Security Council any matter that involves a breach of peace and international security before action is taken, save for self defense; for the United States to take military action in any situation other than limited self-defense without Security Council authorization would amount to a violation of international law.

Community Interests

In QDR 2 through 5, every situation outlined is not only a vital interest to the US but to virtually all nations. Taking the simple one first (QDR 4), access to key markets, etc., I observe that the hundreds of our trading partners have a keen, if not keener, interest in the uninhibited flow of trade than does the US, be it by sea or air; interrupted trade will probably hurt many other nations more than the US As to the freedom of the seas, airways and space (QDR 3), each is covered by international Treaties and Conventions built up over the years. Freedom of the seas and airways and the use of space are of vital interest to virtually every nation. The same applies to preventing the emergence of a hostile regime, regional coalition or hegemony (QDR 2). And, lastly, as to deterring and defeating aggression against friends and allies of the US (QDR 5), once again it is of interest many nations.

The point to be made is that the US appoints itself to enforce international law. On what authority? Whether a unilateral or multilateral approach, in any event it would fall under the aegis of the Security Council.

In the interest of giving you a more detailed look at the QDR it goes on: ". . . the Defense Department has an essential role to play in shaping the international security environment <u>in ways that promote and protect US national interests</u>. . . . the US military serves as a preferred means of engagement with countries that are neither staunch friends or confirmed foes. . . ." And under the heading of Promoting Regional Stability, "<u>Through both example and enforcement, US forces encourage adherence to the international norms</u> (underlining added) and regimes that help provide the foundation for peace and stability around the globe, such as nonproliferation, freedom of navigation, and respect for human rights and rule of law."

In the above underlined phrase, the term "norms" certainly must refer to the law of the jungle, to which I have alluded repeatedly. However if "norms" translates to international law, as stated earlier I see no evidence that US forces intend to abide by international law in enforcing violations of the example given, freedom of navigation. And I'd like to know more about how US *forces* plan to enforce "respect for human rights and rule of law."

Summaries of international sea, airways and space law will be found at the end of this chapter.

As to deterring and defeating aggression against our allies and friends (QDR5), which nations are in our vital interest to defend? Iran, Iraq and North Korea are listed as rogue nations. Certainly there should be no thought of undertaking any of these unilaterally. In this connection, it comes to mind that the US has maintained troops in South Korea for over forty years, numbering 37,000 at the present time. South Korea is just as important to the community of nations as to the US. Why wasn't it a multilateral deterrent force? Why not today?

The adage should be: planning should involve balanced international forces for undertaking major engagements, conducted under Rule of Law and Security Council authorization. I believe that Americans are not willing again to pay the price in lives and treasure as we did in Vietnam. What is called for now are new methods of planning and, yes, multilateral planning. In this connection the

National Review Panel, which critiqued the QDR, stated, "Future Military Success will depend heavily upon the effective joint (Army, Navy, Air) and combined (multinational) operations." Save for the combined planning prior to the Gulf War I see no movement in this direction at this time.

I think Secretary McNamara had it right when he criticized the US involvement in Vietnam—"We did not hold to the principle that US military action—other than in response to direct threats to our own security—should be carried out only in conjunction with multinational forces supported fully [and not merely cosmetically] by the international community."[1] In both Korea and Vietnam only token forces were provided by allies.

Fighting and Winning Wars

In the QDR section on "Fighting and Winning Major Theater Wars (MTW), the high end of crisis continuum is fighting and winning major theater wars . . ." To deter aggression, prevent coercion of allied or friendly governments, and defeat aggression should it occur, we must prepare US forces to confront this scale of threat far from home, in concert with our allies and friends, [aside from post-Iraq operations and the very minor Kosovo operations at the time of writing this, I know of no other such planning] but unilaterally if necessary. . . . it is imperative that the United States . . . be able to deter and defeat large-scale, border-crossing aggression in two distant theaters in over-lapping time frames, preferably in concert with regional allies."

On two-front wars DOD lays out requirements, "The first is being able to rapidly defeat initial enemy advances [like the rapid defeat in Korea and Vietnam?] short of their objectives in two theaters in close succession, one followed almost immediately by another. Maintaining this capability is absolutely critical to the United States ability to seize the initial objective in both theaters and to minimize

[1] "In Retrospect" by Robert McNamara, Copyright Times Books, Random House, Inc., 201 East 50th Street, NY, NY 10022

the amount of territory we and our allies must regain from the enemies. Failure to halt an enemy invasion rapidly can make the subsequent campaign to evict enemy forces from captured territory much more difficult, lengthy and costly. It could also weaken coalition support, undermine US credibility, and increase the risk of conflict elsewhere." The thought of nipping aggression in the bud is a positive and important one. The how of doing it is another matter.

As to the QDR arguments for the "imperative" need for the US to: "fight and win two major wars nearly simultaneously, unilaterally if necessary and possibly on opposite sides of the earth—even withdrawing forces from smaller-scale contingency operations . . . If the United States were to forego its ability to defeat aggression in more than one theater at a time, our standing as a global power, as the security power of choice, and as the leader of the international community would be called into question. Indeed, some allies would read a one-war capability as a signal that the United States, if heavily engaged elsewhere, would no longer be able to defend their interests. Such a capability could also inhibit the United States from responding to a crisis promptly enough, or even at all, for fear of committing the bulk of our forces and making ourselves vulnerable in other regions. This fact is unlikely to escape the attention of potential adversaries. A one-theater war capacity would risk undermining both deterrence and the credibility of US security commitments in key regions of the world. This, in turn, could cause allies and friends to adopt more divergent defense policies and postures, thereby weakening the web of alliances and coalitions on which we rely to protect our interests abroad."

Secretary of Defense Cohen said, "We have determined that US forces must be capable of fighting and winning two major wars nearly simultaneously," a continuation of the Bottom-Up Review policy of 1993. Again, the QDR says we may have to fight them unilaterally. The present candidates to be defeated are listed as: North Korea, Iraq, Iran, Libya and North Korea. Question. Why in the world would the US want to charge off to fight any of these with only token forces provided by allies? And in the first place, why in the world does the US broadcast these nations as rogues—shutting off approaches to ameliorate relations. Later, a proactive policy will be discussed. Further, I'll be labeling them as "rogue-led" nations.

In the Gulf War with Iraq, the US provided the lion's share of the forces, deployed nearly 470,000 thousand troops (most of them to fight a 100 hour land war), was reimbursed $53.7 billion by several nations for doing the fighting (cutting the US cost to about $7 billion), a fact not widely known, making American troops—there is no other name for it—US mercenaries. (Actually, Germany felt it was overcharged and asked for a refund. It wasn't given). Thank God there were few casualties. Had there been many casualties, no doubt there would be an outcry by the bereaved parents heard in Washington. After making this point, I should point out that our military forces performed superbly. President Bush laid the war in the lap of the Security Council. More on this later.

As to an invasion today of South Korea by the North, at this late date why is it in the sole interest of the United States that it take on North Korea unilaterally? The US has done yeoman service in South Korea ever since the war in 1950, but still maintains troops there. Again, many nations have interests in South Korea, particularly in trade. Why are not troops of other nations also there to maintain the peace? As the rogue nations are already identified, why can't combined war planning be undertaken now to make these kinds of wars truly multilateral? One reason the US military is not keen on engaging in multilateral actions is the bother of training with other troops; in spending the time and trouble of coordinating with them, and particularly in communications. The new word for this is "interoperability"—or the lack thereof. Or is our 50-year-old pattern of supplying the vast majority of the troops to places like Korea, Vietnam and the Gulf War going to continue? I don't see any real change, or any multi-lateral war planning, making the QDR quite hollow in this regard.

The QDR goes on, as to "Smaller Scale Contingency Operations (SSC) Operations . . . these operations will still likely pose the most frequent challenge for US forces through 2015 . . ."

As to Shaping Nations

With reference again to "Shaping the International Environment" in ways that promote and protect US interests, not long ago the US went through a siege of trying to shape another nation—

which did not work. "We viewed the people and leaders . . . in terms of our own experience. . . . We totally misjudged the political forces within the country. . . . We underestimated the power of nationalism to motivate the people . . . and we continue to do so in many parts of the world. . . . Our misjudgments of friend and foe alike reflected our profound ignorance of the history, culture, and politics of the people."[1] These words are quoted from Robert McNamara's book, "In Retrospect" and were, of course, on the Vietnam experience. There were similar problems in the early days in South Korea. More wise counsel from Secretary McNamara: "We did not recognize that neither our people nor our leaders are omniscient. Where our own security is not directly at stake, our judgment of what is in another people's or country's interest should be put to the test of open discussion in international forums. We do not have the God-given right to shape every nation in our own image or as we choose." And just how was the US chosen to be the leader of the international community? It's true that many nations look to the US for leadership because of our democratic system. But how did "leader of the international community" get translated to "World Policeman?" Is it the leader because of its military might or for other reasons? And because long ago the US assumed the role of world policeman, it helps to explain why the US spends more money on defense than the next thirteen nations combined. To put it more bluntly, it is the American taxpayer who is paying the bill for our Police Force, for policing the world.

By now most every nation has studied the QDR. Our friends can rest comfortably on their oars. Uncle Sam will take care of most everything. Yes, the US's stated role and its preponderance of forces under its current concepts are a disincentive for other nations to shoulder a larger share of the burden. Conversely, just to dramatize this, if the US provided only a one war capability or two one-half wars capability other nations would see more reason to dig into their pockets for more forces—even deficit finance them, as the US has done for years (remember our current $3.7 trillion debt, created by past wars).

As stated earlier the QDR was masterfully crafted. It touches all the bases. Will the real DOD step forward? Based on past performance the DOD hasn't a great track record on several issues, such as its stand-off on the Gulf War syndrome (the gassing of US troops) and the bloated claims of weapons effectiveness in the Gulf War, which were corrected and significantly reduced in an analysis by the Congressional Budget Office.

The QDR does use language such as the "US forces encourage adherence to international norms and respect for human rights and the rule of law" and lists a number of limited preventive measures, but nowhere do I detect in it any intention of conducting combined war planning with other nations to deal with rogue-led nations or to organize in troublesome regions. I imagine that our like-thinking nations would appreciate DOD shifting to language from "shaping" to "leading." If the US were in their shoes, they would not look kindly at being "shaped." Of course the issue goes much deeper than just language; it reflects the Defense Department's state of mind.

Whenever I hear that word "superpower" the words of Teddy Roosevelt come to mind, "Speak softly and carry a big stick." Wise council then, and now—be strong but act reservedly—or throttle the ego. Rather, I would be gratified if the US took pride in heading the list of nations' infant mortality rates—instead of being about twentieth on the list. (I don't know why that example keeps popping into my head). Or heading the worldwide scholarship list. Recall that President Bush called for an kinder, gentler, world.

Highly placed government officials refer frequently to that title, "superpower" or "the only superpower," as the foremost description of the United States. To me those monikers have more negative implications and innuendoes than positive. What message are they trying to send? It seems to me that it is a threat, if veiled, not only to rogues, but to friends, too. Does it connote that we're the toughest boy on the block? Does it imply that we will solve our friends problems, inferring that we'll do it on our own terms and in our own way. Do they send the message that the US is a militaristic society? How will this awesome power be used?

Having said all this, we should be grateful—quietly—that the US is strong, that it is endowed with its form of government, widely admired and oft emulated in the world, and that it is generous. Nonetheless, we need be vigilant that this awesome power is not misused. President Eisenhower put it this way "Only an alert and knowledgeable citizenry can compel the proper meshing of the huge industrial and military machinery of defense with our peaceful methods and goals, so that security and liberty will prosper together." Today, we are not meshed.

The thesis of the QDR continues the eons-old practice of one nation against another, a bloc of nations taking on another bloc. As the rogue-led nations have been identified, the US should take the lead in developing balanced, combined (international) war plans with each nation providing its share of forces, much as was done in the several years before the Gulf War. Moreover, an astute diplomatic campaign could ameliorate the situation meaningfully.

Note that President Bush laid the Gulf War in the lap of the Security Council. Eleven resolutions were issued—the first within hours after Saddam Hussein's aggression began—authorizing the response and then putting him in a straitjacket.

None of what has been said above should be interpreted as needing less than topnotch military forces in appropriate mix and quantity.

In view of all the serious issues raised herein with respect to military policy, strategy and planning to the year 2015, I propose that the President appoint a very select panel, reflecting all views, to address them. A supremely important issue is whether it is in the interest of the United States to continue to conduct its affairs in the age-old jungle ways—or to shift to my proposed Rule of Law.

As to Prevention

Preventive measures addressed in the QDR include efforts to:

"Actually reduce or eliminate NBC (nuclear, biological and chemical) capabilities, as has been done with the US—North Korean Agreed Framework and the Cooperative Threat Reduction program with Russia, Ukraine, Belarus, and Kazakhstan.

Discourage arms races and proliferation of NBC weapons, as is being done by DOD efforts to monitor and enforce arms control agreements, such as the Nuclear Non-Proliferation Treaty and the Missile Technology Control Regime, and others.

Our nuclear posture also contributes substantially to our ability to deter aggression in peacetime." (Note that Saddam Hussein ignored our stockpile of weapons when he undertook his aggression into Kuwait).

The United States must retain nuclear forces sufficient to deter any hostile foreign leadership . . . and remains committed to negotiating further reductions . . . consistent with the agreed START III framework once Russia's Duma ratifies the START II Treaty."

For those interested in the pertinent detail of international law, following are quotes on the Treaties and Conventions applicable to the seas•, air•• and space•••.

• The principle of the freedom of the seas was established by consistent maritime practice during the last two centuries after the major naval powers had abandoned the policy of closed seas and successfully secured free navigation to all parts of the world for the purposes of their trade, their fisheries and the protection of nationals.

   The freedom of the high seas and the rights of the States flowing therefrom with respect to the free use of the high seas and its resources have since been universally recognized as part of customary international law and codified in the Convention of the High Seas of April 29, 1958 and Arts. 86 to 115 of the United Nations Convention of the Law of the Sea of December 10, 1982.

•• Air law is layered with bilateral and multilateral accords: the 1944 Chicago Convention on International Civil Aviation is first of all the constitution of the International Civil Aviation Organization (ICAO)—a United Nations Specialized Agency, designed above all to foster the safe and orderly development of civil aviation, membership in which is now almost universal.

   The increased tide of unlawful interference with international civil aviation from the late 1960s onward prompted the ICAO Council . . . to initiate . . . treaties dealing with the situation: the 1970 Hague Convention . . . with highjacking; the 1971 Montreal Convention . . . with sabotage; the 1988 Montreal Protocol for the Suppression of violence at airports. . . . The aim of the treaties is to deprive the culprit of the offenses in question of a safe haven. . . . Meanwhile, ICAO remains the principal forum for the development of international air law, and through it, domestic air laws.

The three principal Conventions have been ratified by a large majority. There is a growing tendency to hold that acts constituting interference with international civil aviation affects the interests of the world community and must be suppressed whatever the situation or the motive of the offender.

••• In 1958, the United Nations General Assembly created an ad hoc committee on Peaceful Uses of Outer Space, resulting in the 1967 Outer Space Treaty and reaffirmed by the 1979 Moon and Celestial Body Treaty (Moon Treaty). The latter provides that "States Parties to the Treaty undertake not to place in orbit around the earth any objects carrying nuclear weapons or any other kinds of weapons of mass destruction, such as weapons on celestial bodies, or station such weapons in outer space in any other manner. The Moon and any other celestial bodies shall be used by all States Parties to the Treaty exclusively for peaceful purposes.

The growing danger of militarization of outer space can hardly be overestimated. The Outer Space Treaty provides only for partial demilitarization of outer space. The advent of the new technologies such as anti-satellite (ASATS) ballistic missile defense (BMD) and strategic defense initiative (SDI) systems will require not only clarification of existing rules, but also of new legal instruments and possible compromise to limit and reduce such activities.

17

Rule of Law

It may seem odd that a person who spent years in the military service is writing on Rule of Law. It is. But maybe it's a boon to the thinking reader, as it's written in layman's language—not in legalese.

It just so happens the Rule of Law is at the center of what follows. So here goes: For millennia, bands of people, tribes and nations have acted in accordance with their own self-interest. Every reason imaginable has been used to aggress another's territory or area for many reasons or pretexts: food, prestige, fear, greed, avarice, expansion room, ideology, retaliation, jealously, raw materials, slaves, women, and on and on.

The League of Nations was an attempt to civilize the conduct of nations. It failed for lack of enforcing mechanisms. Twenty-five years and one World War later (again, the bloodiest war ever) a new organization, the United Nations, was created by the 51 nations represented in San Francisco at the close of WW II. Arthur Vandenberg led the US bipartisan group in its establishment. Now, with 184 member nations, virtually the entire world is represented, reflecting the hunger for peace and security.

The UN Charter

When I first read the Preamble to the Charter I was thrilled. It reminded me of our Declaration of Independence and our Constitution, which so many have emulated or envied. The Preamble starts: "WE THE PEOPLES OF THE UNITED NATIONS, DETERMINED . . .

to save succeeding generations from the scourge of war, which twice in our lifetime has brought untold sorrow to mankind . . ."

Its purpose, "To maintain or restore international peace and security . . ."

The founders of the United Nations had something revolutionary in mind: replace the age-old self-interest ways of relating to each other with the Rule of Law. In my terms, instead of the old 'us' vs. 'them' ways or one 'bloc' of nations against another 'bloc', the founders foresaw it as the 'law-abiding' vs. 'outlaws'. A profound change, if you think on it. Rule of Law has been millions of years in the coming which may help explain why it has been so slow to catch hold. For more than fifty years after the UN's inception, many nations, including our own, have not realized its potential. But isn't Rule of Law the way individual civilized nations maintain peace and security, by protecting law-abiding citizens from outlaws? And isn't it Rule of Law, together with our democratic form of government, what made the United States great? President Eisenhower put it this way, "The world no longer has a choice between force and law. If civilization is to survive, it must choose Rule of Law."

During his presidency he recommended to the UN Secretary-General that a UN Peace Force be established, a force that is specifically required in the UN Charter. It has not yet materialized; it is long overdue. (In a general sense the US has seen fit to substitute for it—for reasons that will become clear). I am a great admirer of General Eisenhower, not only for his generalship but as a great person, rising from simple means. President Bush, another man who came through the fire of war, on the eve of the Gulf War seconded this thinking in an address to Congress on the eve of the Gulf War saying, "We have before us the opportunity to forge ourselves and for future generations a new world order, a world order where rule of law, not the rule of the jungle, governs the conduct of nations." Neither president has yet been heard. Even I got into the act. From my 1988 book I quote myself, "The United States should capitalize on the new enlightenment in the world by dedicating itself to taking the lead in bringing into being an effective world security arrangement, a world governed by law." (Note that Presidents Eisenhower and Bush were Republicans. The reason for mentioning this now will become apparent).

The Security Council

Now to the Security Council. It has fifteen members, the Permanent Five members, Britain, China, France, Russia, and the US; the other ten are rotating members. Under consideration at the moment is a move to add Germany and Japan as permanent members and another to increase the Council to eighteen members. My principal concern is that there be an odd number of members. The reason will become clear.

I am somewhat reluctant to do this but I'm going to quote several selected articles of the Charter to show, inter alia, the Security Council's functions and responsibilities, which are the core, the heartbeat of the United Nations. Indeed, its decisions are, in fact, international law. I overcame my reluctance because in talks I have given to informed people I've asked for a show of hands of those who had read the Charter. The response: virtually nil. I've underlined to highlight the key points. I've pared the quotes to a minimum to provide a basic foundation.

Chapter 6

Pacific Settlement of Disputes

Art, 33.(1) The parties to any dispute whose continuance is likely to endanger the maintenance of international peace and security shall, first of all, seek a solution of international peace and security by negotiation, inquiry, mediation, conciliation, arbitration, judicial settlement, resort to regional agencies and arrangements, or other peaceful means of their own choice.

(2) The Security Council shall, when it deems necessary, call upon the parties to settle their disputes by such means, etc.

Chapter 7

Action with Respect to Treats to the Peace,

Breaches of the Peace

Acts of Aggression

Art. 39. <u>The Security Council shall determine the existence of any threat to the peace, breach of the peace or act of aggression, and shall make recommendations, or decide what measures shall be taken in</u> accordance with Art. 41 and 42, to maintain or restore international peace and security.

Art. 40. In order to prevent an aggravation of such situation, the Security Council may, before making the recommendations or deciding upon measures provided for in Art. 41, call upon the parties concerned to comply with such provisional measures as it deems necessary or desirable. Such provisional measures shall be without prejudice to the rights, claims or position of the parties concerned. The Security Council shall take account of failure to comply with such provisional measures.

Art. 41. <u>The Security Council may decide what measures not involving the use of armed force are to be employed</u> to give effect to its decisions, and many call upon members of the United Nations to apply such measures. These may include complete or partial interruption of economic relations and of rail, sea, air, postal, telegraphic, radio and other means of communication, and the severance of diplomatic relations.

Art. 42. Should <u>the Security Council</u> consider that measures provided in Art. 41 would be inadequate, or have proved to be inadequate, it <u>may take such actions by air, sea or land forces as may be necessary to maintain or restore international peace and security.</u> Such actions may include demonstrations, blockade, and other operations by air, sea or land forces of members of the United Nations.

Art. 43.(1) <u>All members</u> of the United Nations, in order to contribute the maintenance of international peace and security, <u>undertake to make available to the Security Council</u> on its call and in accordance with a special agreement or agreements, <u>armed forces, assistance and facilities, including rights of passage,</u> necessary for the purpose of maintaining international peace and security.

(2) <u>Such agreement or agreements shall govern the numbers and type of forces, their degree of readiness and general location, and the nature of the facilities and assistance to be provided.</u>

(3) <u>The agreement or agreements shall be negotiated as soon as possible</u> on the initiative of the Security Council and member states or between the Security Council and groups of member states, and shall be subject to ratification by the signatory states.

Art. 45. <u>In order to enable the United Nations to take urgent military measures, members shall hold immediately available national air force contingents for combined international enforcement action.</u> The strength and degree of readiness of these contingents, and plans for their combined action, shall be determined, within the limits laid down in the special agreement or agreements referred to in Art. 43, by the Security Council with the assistance of the Military Staff Committee.

Art. 51. <u>Nothing in the present Charter shall impair the right of individual or collective self-defense,</u> if an armed attack occurs against a member of the organization, until the Security Council has taken the measures necessary to maintain international peace and security. . . ."

Regional Arrangements

"Chapter 8

Art. 52.(1) <u>Nothing in the present Charter precludes the existence of regional arrangements or agencies for dealing with such matters relating to the maintenance of international peace and security</u> as are appropriate for regional action, provided that such arrangements or agencies and their activities and their activities are consistent with the purposes and principles of the organization. . . .

Art 53.(1) The Security Council shall, where appropriate, utilize such arrangements or agencies for enforcement action under its authority. But <u>no enforcement action shall be taken under regional</u>

arrangements or by regional agencies without the authorization of
the Security Council. . . ."

The basic structure of the UN has been in place since 1945 but
unfortunately, due to the Soviet veto or the threat thereof in the Security Council for forty-five years of the Cold War and the Soviet-
US arms race, the structure has not been manned or utilized as
prescribed. Critical planning has not been done. Even today the Military Staff Committee, composed of the senior military officers of the
Permanent Five, has never functioned. Without military advice the
Council is like the US without the Pentagon. Nor have member states
entered into the prescribed agreements for the use of their forces in
combat situations; the Security Council still has no agreements with
nations on commitment of forces for use under Articles 41 through
45. Eisenhower's Peace force, proposed over forty years ago, has not
been constituted.

As discussed earlier, in the case of the 1991 Gulf War, the US
having planned for just such a situation for several years, requested
and secured a resolution which was approved by all members of the
Security Council—including Russia—to authorize repelling Saddam Hussein's forces from Kuwait. It was no doubt that President
Bush, having been US Representative to the UN and familiar with
the Security Council, chose to seek authority to act under the UN
rather than winging it alone. In all, there were eleven resolutions, all
agreed by Russia, in just the first ten days of the war. This matter will
be continued in the Chapter 10 on Fixing the Security Council.

Earlier I referred to the dichotomy existing between the White
House and Department of Defense (DOD) with the UN Security Council. Interesting, that their policy documents issued in 1997—which set
policy to the year 2015—make no mention of the United Nations or
the Security Council, yet worked hand-in-hand with the Security
Council and the Secretary-General over Saddam's intransigence in
1998. Confusing isn't it? It's time for the US to set a firm course.

With reference to the previous chapter the terms of Article 39
of the UN Charter would seem clearly to cover any nation, for example, interfering with the freedom of the sea lines of communica-

tion, airways, and space for instance. While they are listed also in the QDR as US vital interests, warranting, if considered necessary, possible US military intervention (note that all three are already regulated by international law), under Article 39 the Security Council is obligated to make recommendations, or *decide* what measures to take, thus precluding a nation from taking unilateral military action, except in self defense, of course. Thus, any nation which takes military action beyond self defense would clearly contravene the UN Charter, placing it in the category of a rogue nation. Of all nations, because of its stature and power, the US needs to set the example by abiding scrupulously with the Charter and other international law. However, as an example the US missile attacks in 1998 against Afghanistan and Sudan in retaliation for the bombing of the embassy would seem clearly a violation of Article 39.

I am just as concerned as anyone that US vital interests be met. There are lawful ways to accomplish these.

Gradually, but quite slowly, Rule of Law is becoming the rule. The Gulf War set a precedent of sorts for dealing with conflict, with aggression. During the life of the UN over 300 treaties, conventions, protocols and the like have been created, covering a wide range of international behavior.

The US by taking the lead in advancing Rule of Law, will do a great service for the world; it is the only nation that can bring it about. Knowing my country, the moment it decides to take the lead in making the UN what it was intended to be it will go all out, to not only initiate codification of international law, but to implement and enforce it.

The International Criminal Court

The Nuremberg War Crimes Tribunal which convicted World War ll war criminals set the precedent, yet any war criminals in Bosnia were not brought to justice for lack of an adequate basis to do so.

My longtime friend, Benjamin Ferencz, a chief prosecutor at the Nuremberg trials, has devoted all his time for several years to the creation of an International Criminal Court—his dream of over fifty years. In a recent article he said "Pressed by public outrage, the

Security Council was able, in a few months time, to approve statutes for ad hoc criminal tribunals to punish crimes against humanity in the former Yugoslavia and Ruwanda . . . But the Permanent Five, for unstated reasons, failed to create an enforcement mechanism."[1] I note that Saddam Hussein has not been indicted, tried or punished for his aggression into Kuwait; his people have suffered under Security Council sanctions, but not Saddam.

Ferencz goes on. "Nations should recognize that a more peaceful and humane world can only come about by replacing the force of war by the force of law. Small and poor nations have more at stake than the rich and powerful. On our interdependent planet, the peace and well-being of each is inextricably linked to the peace and well-being of all. Outdated notions of sovereignty must not block acceptance of the rules of the road needed to enhance the security of people everywhere by deterring wars of aggression, genocide and horrible crimes against humanity that continue to deface the human landscape.

"Enforcement remains a problem. Without force, law is a farce. . . . although the UN Charter called for an international military force to maintain peace, the mandates have not yet been honored. Consent by the five permanent members is required before the Council can impose economic, military or other sanctions.

"The [UN] General Assembly has instructed a Preparatory Committee to draft a constitution . . . for consideration by high-ranking diplomats tentatively set to take place in Italy in June 1998."[1]

Imagine what the International Criminal Court could accomplish! Megalomaniacs such as Stalin, Tojo, and Hitler would have known in advance that they would face consequences such as hanging or imprisonment, the sentences which were imposed at Nuremberg. Hitler, of course, couldn't face his fate; he took his own life. A track record of such punishments should sober even the most adventurous paranoid—much more so the relatively sane leaders who commit war crimes—thus creating a powerful deterrent.

While writing this, on July 17, 1998 the long-awaited International Criminal Court (ICC) Statute came into being, providing for

[1] Benjamin Ferencz, in the Journal of the Nuclear Age Peace Foundation

the punishment of those guilty of war crimes, genocide, and crimes against humanity. 120 nations, including all nations in Europe, voted "yea;" six nations including China, Israel, Iraq, Libya, and notably the United States, dissented. The Statute will stay open for signature in New York until December 31, 2000. Why did the President of the United States choose to dissent—and at the last minute?

According to Adrian Karatnycky, President of Freedom House, "At root, the new court reflects the view held by many in the international elite that more power should be ceded to international institutions. Most Americans—and not only Jesse Helms, who has steadfastly opposed the court out of concern over the erosion of US sovereignty—realize that much of the world does not share our values and so are skeptical of such transfers of authority will understand that a US force free to act constructively and decisively abroad is essential for ensuring peace and for expanding and protecting freedom. . . . Such laudable aims can be assured only through the thoughtful actions of a democratic superpower that can strategically apply its military power in dangerous settings.

"In the end, the International Criminal Court will no more eliminate genocide and war crimes than the establishment of the United Nations ushered in an era of cooperation and fraternity among nations. Such laudable aims can be assured only through the thoughtful actions of a democratic superpower that can strategically apply its military power in dangerous settings."[2]

The above statement crystallizes the issue facing the America and the world—is it to be a continuation of the law of the jungle or Rule of Law? Think back on the US role as world policeman—Korea, Vietnam? Remember Secretary McNamara's sound advice on Vietnam—after the fact. Mr. Karatnycky, why not democratic nations operating under the Security Council to enforce international law—rather than promoting ones own self-serving agenda? In any event—whether it be done unilaterally or if it be multilateral action under the Security Council—the ICC will deter, 'tyrants, aggressors and perpetrators of ethnic cleansing,' and probably more so if the authority of the Security Council is involved. And as a final point, no single Senator should have the power to control the decision on this core issue for the US and the world. Thank you for making the issues so clear.

[2] Karatnycky, President of Freedom House

And does this remind you of the thesis of the White House and the Defense Department's Quadrennial Review, which provides for two major wars fought nearly simultaneously—or any military action. But which are permissible only with the Security Council's authorization? Recall that the US has been a self-proclaimed world policeman, for which the American people pay the bill—or it taps other nations to pay, making US troops hired mercenaries. Again I ask, why? Here's another view by George Melloan who says "The hard work of trying to maintain some semblance of order in the world falls elsewhere, to the major democracies, especially the United States. [Not so! Melloan should read the UN Charter]. The US voted against the Rome treaty not because it opposes its goals. Quite the contrary, the US has favored such a body for years. But hardheaded realists in the administration, particularly in the Pentagon, knew that the US unlike some other signatories, would feel bound by its terms" [So the US military can freewheel, to do anything it wishes and not be bound by rules required on others? The double standard again, Maybe, too, the President is concerned that charges could be made by the ICC against him—for an escapade like Panama City]. "And they, along with Jesse Helms, feared that those terms would make it harder, not easier, to maintain peace and order in the world." [Again, the double standard. A crime is a crime no matter who commits it.]

"The US military operates throughout the world, ready to bring pressure to bear on countries that threaten US interests. In most cases, those interests are identical with those of other democratic nations and with all nations that want to conduct normal activities, such as trade, in a peaceful international environment. This is about the only peacekeeping effort that exists today."[3] [That can—and must— be changed].

Whoa! There's that ego again. Apply military pressure—and for trade? What happens when other nations apply military pressure on the US—for whatever reason? What sort of world does this engender? It's this sort of policy that fuels arms races, and wars. There

[3] Melloan, "Don't Worry War Criminals, The New Court Won't Work," Wall Street Journal 7-26-98. Republication by permission of Dow Jones, Inc. via Copyright Clearance Center, Inc. (C) 1998, Dow Jones and Company, Inc. All rights reserved.

probably would have been more had the US paid its dues, which are in arrears mostly because of peacekeeping operations.

Benjamin Ferencz, that Prosecutor at the Nuremberg trials, who has argued for over fifty years for an international criminal court, reacts to George Melloan's article. He provided the Wall Street Journal with the following article for publication on the day following Melloan's. *It was not published.*

"George Melloan reluctantly concurs with our government's refusal to accept an International Criminal Court. None of the reasons given to justify US recalcitrance is persuasive.

"The tribunal will be an independent judiciary of carefully selected, highly qualified judges and the prosecutors will be subject to judicial, budgetary and administrative controls as well as public scrutiny. There is no way the General Assembly of the United Nations can convert the Court into a political tool that might oppress Americans. The assumptions that the Court may be dominated by 'troublemakers and tyrants' is unjustified. Our experience at Nuremberg, Tokyo, and the international criminal courts we recently helped establish to deal with war crimes against humanity in Yugoslavia and Rwanda proves the opposite.

"It is argued that humanitarian action by the United States might be dampened by the existence of an international criminal court. Possibly, but unilateral military intervention, without Security Council approval, is both illegal and dangerous. A self-appointed sheriff, even with a posse, is not a cherished institution. No one authorized the United States to be the world's policeman. Our military is safer to rely on law rather than war.

"The new tribunal can act only if national jurisdictions are unable or unwilling to try offenders fairly. The US is not bound unless two-thirds of the Senate ratifies the treaty. There is no retroactivity. Only genocide, crimes against humanity, major war crimes and possibly aggression can be considered by the court—crimes that invariably require complicity by a state. To argue that the state should have to consent before any of its nationals can be put on trial for such horrendous crimes makes mockery of the rule of law. Without an international court such crimes might never be published.

"It pained me to see the United States humiliated in Rome by the overwhelming rejection of its unpersuasive arguments. The

United States should re-think its position and lend its leadership and support to the new International Criminal Court. The best way to protect our brave young people in the military, as well as people everywhere, is to rely on the force of law rather than the law of force."[4]

What a shame that the American people did not have the opportunity to read Ferencz' article.

In the 1998 Summer Edition of *The Interdependent,* published by the United Nations Association of the USA, John Washburn said, "The United States deserves credit for the high quality of important parts of the Statute as well as blame for some of its most serious defects. The professional quality, hard work, and personal ability of the US delegation would have done the United States proud had the outcome not been such a fiasco.

"In the end, Washington could not accept anything less than a total guarantee that no American, and especially, no American military person, would ever be tried by the Court. For the Court that must be universal in a world of sovereign states, an exemption for any one country would be an exemption for all. Practically, that would have meant that very few, if any, cases would reach the Court other than referrals from the Security Council. The great majority of the Conference were willing to compromise a long way in this direction, and seriously restricted the Court as a result: but they could not and would not go as far as the United States wanted."[5]

Another cogent view on the ICC by William A. Collins, a former state representative from Connecticut, "Being the world's only superpower allows one to assume a fairly arbitrary stance toward justice. Take Jesse Helms. He recently put forth the US Senate view of the new international war crime tribunal. He assured us that the Senate would never ratify it if any American could ever be prosecuted under it's terms. . . . .and we displayed similar arrogance in Manila, where the Philippines and the US administrations signed a Visiting Forces agreement. Under it Filipino troops who commit crimes over here, will be tried over here. But Americans who com-

---

[4] Benjamin Ferencz, furnished as a courtesy.
[5] *The Interdependent,* Summer Edition, 1998, published by the UN Association of the USA.

mit crimes over there, will also be tried over here . . . But American behavior in this little dustup was peanuts compared to [ICC] war crimes proceedings. In the end, the vote affirming the creation of the court was 120 to 6. [The US, one of the six] . . . The rest of our allies voted against us in disgust . . . Throughout those proceedings, the United States used its muscle to oppose provisions that would make it next to impossible for any Western nation, especially us, to be prosecuted . . . But the delegates didn't buy that, so we tried another tack. We insisted that every prosecution be first approved by the UN Security Council. That would allow us to veto any embarrassing ones. That lost too, 113-17.

"And so, in the end, we voted "no" on the whole shebang. We claimed that American troops, scattered abroad on so many peace-keeping missions, would be too vulnerable to politically motivated accusations. Unkind observers pointed out, however, that compared to other nations, the US is rather chintzy in its contribution of such troops.

"Unspoken, but understood, was our far greater fear. The other players all knew that what really worried us was the potential for much more serious allegations. These include our invasion of Panama and Grenada, our unilateral bombing of Libya and Baghdad (and now Khartoum and Afghanistan) and our attempted assassinations of sundry world leaders.

"After all, what's the point of being the world's only super power if you have to stand trial for your misdeeds, just like everybody else?"[6]

The United States has until December 31, 2000 to sign on to the Statute of the International Criminal Court. I pray that it does—and soon.

Again the US has displayed an arrogance that prevents constructive dialogue with our neighbors on this planet, and yes, triggering animosity from friends as well as foes. Other examples are present in Chapters 16, 18 and 19.

---

[6] ICC by William A. Collins, Charlottesville,VA. Daily Progress, 10-4-98, courtesy the Associated Press

Instead, US fostering and helping—and, yes, taking the lead—in establishing worldwide Rule of Law would alter radically for the better this hostile and turbulent world. The US is the only nation that can get away with these types of actions—and the only nation that can lead to the consummation of worldwide Rule of Law.

I note that both Karatnycky and Melloan argue for the continuation of the role of world policeman for America in their articles appearing in the Wall Street Journal just two days apart. I note, too, that the major beneficiary of continuing the world policeman role is the US military-industrial complex, selling arms to our government, as well as nations world-wide. (I hear you, President Eisenhower). Is it just a coincidence that the Wall Street Journal, interested primarily in commerce, finance and profits, promotes this concept? And by this, foregoing instituting of worldwide Rule of Law, which has the enormous potential of saving not only American lives and their taxes, and as well, the security of nations worldwide.

18

The United States, World Leader or Rogue Nation?

Some years ago the United States was tagged with the title, Leader of the Free World; the leader of democratic and moderately socialistic nations as opposed to Communist or totalitarian systems. But things changed. In 1990 Vaclav Havel caught the change, "People have passed through the very dark tunnel at the end of which there was a light of freedom. Unexpectedly they passed through the prison gates and found themselves in a square. They are now free and they don't know where to go."[1]

The basic policies of the United States haven't adjusted; the White House hasn't fully recognized it—and doesn't know where to go. Yet the responsibility resides in the Office of the President, which is charged in the Constitution with responsibility for foreign policy. I might add, that Congress has not made a contribution either.

It hasn't yet really sunk in that the world is no longer polarized, that the Soviet Union no longer exists, that Russia is a democracy, though a struggling one. Expanding NATO in Russia's direction wasn't a friendly act. To the contrary, it just may delay or even derail US-Russian arms reductions, prolonging the all-important nuclear threat, or worse, push Russia back into a totalitarian regime, thus reviving the only threat that could do serious harm to the United States. China is becoming a thriving market economy, appears to be giving attention to human rights, and currently threatens no nation. The world is linked ever-closer daily by trade and communication.

---

[1] Columbia Dictionary of Quotes, Columbia University Press

Still, there are local threats by a handful of nations, which cry for a solution.

Following is a series of rogue, or roguish, actions taken by the United States in the recent past. A definition of a rogue nation: a nation acting in violation of international law.

1. Mining Nicaraguan Ports. "The US CIA admitted (1984) directing the mining of Nicaraguan ports," which the International Court of Justice in the Hague ruled as an illegal act of aggression.[2]

2. Libya. "In 1986 the US President ordered the bombing of Qaddaffi's headquarters in Tripoli in retaliation for the bombing of a discotheque in West Berlin that killed one American soldier and a Turkish woman, wounding 230. A US F-111 with two airmen was lost in the attack. Three hostages were killed in Lebanon in reprisal for the US attack."[2A]

3. "In 1989 Panama's voters ousted Manuel Antonio Noriega in free elections May 7. Noriega ignores the election results and retains power, he quells an attempted military coup October 3. The Bush administration comes under fire for not giving the rebels support. Noriega's National Assembly declares war on December 15 and formalizes Noriega's position as head of state. An unarmed US army officer is killed December 16, a Navy officer and his wife are harassed and US airborne troops invade Panama December 20, offering a $1 million reward for information leading to Noriega's arrest. As many as 4,000 Panamanian civilians are killed (Washington says 202), and 23 US servicemen are killed. Other Latin countries express outrage at the US invasion; the UN General Assembly denounces it as a 'flagrant violation of international law.' Noriega eludes capture, turns himself in to Vatican authorities in Panama City December 24,

---

[2] Reprinted with permission from The World Almanac and Book of Facts 1995, Copyright 1995, PRIMEDIA Reference, Inc. One International Blvd. Suite 630, Mahway, NJ 07495. All rights reserved.

[2A] The Peoples Chronicle, licensed by Henry Holt and Company, Inc. Copyright by James Trager. All rights reserved.

and receives political asylum for 10 days before surrendering to US authorities for trial at Miami on drug charges."[2A]

4. The CIA in Iraq. For a number of years the CIA was actively engaged in deposing Saddam Hussein, among others. David Wurmser, Director for the Middle East, American Enterprise Institute reports that, "Two coup attempts exemplified US failure. . . . and efforts to oust Saddam via a coup have failed so many times. . . . At one point, the US supported such an insurgency. . . . It reached a peak when INC (Iraq National Congress) troops invaded Iraqi territory . . . with impunity absorbing thousands of defecting Iraqi soldiers along the way. . . . But the US never recognized the INC as the provisional government of Iraq. . . . Worse, the US abandoned the INC at the pinnacle of success in 1995. US officials assumed that the broad-based upheaval in Iraq . . . would so humiliate and threaten the military establishment that the coup planners would rally behind Saddam."

Wurmser goes on, "Washington's consistent preference for a coup over a broad-based revolution illustrates a deeper theme underlying US policy in the Middle East. The US has traditionally aimed at the institution of tyranny. . . . The current impasse imposes demands that Washington reexamine its entire approach to the Middle East. Washington was no choice now but to abandon the coup option and resurrect the INC . . . There is no cost-free way to depose Saddam. He is more resolute, wily and brutal than we."[3]

I gather the inference is that the US should be more resolute, wily and brutal than he. (I couldn't resist the opportunity). Actually, I commend David Wurmser for bringing all this to the light of day.

Americans have been aware all along that the CIA has been in the dirty tricks business. But these exposés are the most finite example I've run across. It is time to examine the CIA's entire role. Granted that Saddam Hussein is a rogue, a despot, and a megalomaniac, but after attacks to depose him there is little wonder that he

---

[3] David Wurmser, Resident Fellow, American Enterprise Institute, reprint permission, copyright 1997, printed in the Wall Street Journal, November 12, 1997.

focuses his anger at the US and specifically at the Americans in the UN inspection team. The CIA's actions lays the US open to vengeful retaliation—by any nation so treated—including the possible use of a mass destruction suitcase neutron bomb or one of lethal chemicals and if mad enough, placed at the front door of the White House. Why is it that the US appoints itself such roles? How would the US react if some nation was discovered attempting to depose our president? We can depose the head of another nation, yet one of our political parties has made a furor over accepting even money from overseas—to influence an election. What a double standard!

If we are ever to overcome our ancient animosities, the institution of genuine Rule of Law is essential. The very nature of the CIA's role is antithetical in today's world. The United States cannot, in this era be two-faced, be on both sides of the law. If the US is to be an example to the world, the leader of the world community, its actions needs be scrupulous at all times. The worldwide role of the CIA needs a major review in light of the New Strategy for America. "The United States has violated the Chemical Weapons Convention since it was ratified 18 months ago and could undermine the treaty's regime for inspecting poison gas facilities around the world unless the Congress soon passes implementing legislation. . . . ,"according to Washington Post's Staffer Vernon Loeb. "Congress and the Clinton administration have allowed implementing legislation to languish while adding provisions that could 'gut' the treaty's international control and inspection system. . . . The Clinton administration . . . has also reneged on promises to provide the treaty's international governing body with training and equipment, has failed to pay $5.5 million in dues . . . and has refused to cooperate fully with inspectors visiting US facilities . . ."[4]

What to say? Just another case of ego-itis. Our government wants other nations to toe the mark, but it operates by its own rules—in spite of giving its word, thus depreciating its word. Doesn't this raise the question with all nations, why bother to negotiate with the US?

And on the heels of the Chemical Weapon Convention matter comes a new bombshell, the UN fiasco.

[4] Vernon Loeb, Copyright 1988, **[The Washington Post, September 17, 1997, Reprinted with permission.]**

Dan Smith, a retired Army Colonel with the Center for Defense Information reported that "September 21, 1998 is the first day of the general debate of the 53rd annual United Nations General Assembly meeting. It may well be the most fateful session for the United States in the UN's history.

"Considering that the United Nations was created in large measure because of US leadership, one can only be appalled when contemplating the current state of US-UN relations. The President, who is scheduled to speak to the General Assembly on its opening day, comes before world representatives who see the most powerful nation in the world seemingly bent on destroying the UN's ability to operate effectively on a broad array of issues.

"The most pressing issue for the President and the UN is US arrears. As of the end of July 1998, the US owes the UN approximately $1.5 billion for unpaid assessments for regular UN operations and UN peacekeeping missions.

"The President submitted a supplemental budget request of just over $1.02 billion for the current fiscal year [which ends September 30] to pay off at least some of the arrears to the UN and other international organizations). This request has been stalled by those in Congress who do not believe that the reforms implemented by the UN Secretary General are enough.

"Regular Fiscal Year 1999 funding for the UN has fared no better. Funds for the current year's assessments are part of the State Department's Appropriation, one of 13 funding bills still tied up in the Congress. The congressional action cutting peacekeeping funds is perhaps the most short-sighted of all. The UN's peacekeeping missions relieve the US of the need to deploy large numbers of troops to help sustain cease-fires and oversee implementation of peace accords in sixteen locations around the globe—and do so at a bargain price. Of the 14,453 peacekeepers currently employed around the world, only 529 are Americans.

"Our failure to fully pay our share of UN operations costs will soon become an issue that goes beyond mere money. Article 19 of the UN Charter says that a nation's right to vote in the General Assembly can be denied if its arrears equal or exceed the amount of the contributions due from it for the preceding two full years. The United States, the world's richest nation, will be at this point in 1999.

Not to do so would set a deplorable precedent and damage the UN far more than the enforcing the provision—even against the world's only remaining superpower.

"What is perhaps most frustrating about this whole situation is that Congress is ignoring the wishes of the American public. Polls show that Americans understand the importance of the UN and support it and its work.

"Continued failure to appropriate money for current UN operations and to pay our nation's arrears is inexcusable and undercuts the valuable work of the UN. Congress in this case should heed, not obstruct, the American public."[5]

At press time, the House is considering paying about 80% of outstanding bills and reducing annual fees by 20%.

In all fairness, this nation of ours has been at times most benevolent and supportive of other nations. Just a short list of examples is provided to give a balance—although now historical:

1. The first that comes to mind is the organization of the Combined Berlin Airlift; the first, I imagine, because I was a part of it, as was indicated earlier in the book. Yes, it was a stroke of genius, feeding the starving Berliners who were caught between two sets of powers, The Soviet Union and the Allies. In all 2.3 million tons of food, fuel, machinery and supplies were flown to Berlin in 277,000 flights. I see the spirit of the airlift as a precursor of the current democracy in Germany.

2. The Marshall Plan or European Recovery Program was first urged by US Secretary of State in June, 1947, to foster European economic recovery after World War II. America dispensed $12 billion in aid, providing a shot in the arm for many nations.

3. More recently, during the worldwide economic fiascoes, the United States has been generous in supporting financially

[5] From an article in the Washington-based Center for Defense Information's Weekly Defense Monitor, by Dan Smith, Colonel, US Army (Ret.), owner-weekly@mail.cdi.org

several nations, including Russia, Brazil and by providing $18 billion to the International Monetary Fund to strengthen these and more of the world's economies.

4. And, yes, the US was a principal prime mover in the creation of the United Nations and of NATO.

5. Also, for some time the US has been the honest broker in the troubled Mideast.

World War ll was the shining hour for America. Americans, acting as one, went all-out to defeat tyranny. I was proud to be a part of it.

America, leading the world into Rule of Law, would be its shining hour at the beginning of the 21st Century. I want to witness it, to take part in it. But I'll be 81 at the turn of the century. My father passed on at 80, my mother at near 97, so there isn't much time. The United States has a long way to go to bring to pass worldwide Rule of Law. It is the only nation that can bring it about. It has to shift gears, to adopt new policies, and to embrace a new strategy, to prevent wars.

I look forward to witnessing the world celebration marking the end of three million years in the jungle and the beginning of genuine worldwide Rule of Law—together with its means of enforcement and preventive measures.

19

How Does Our Government Operate?

There are three principal policy players in the executive branch of our government with interests in external affairs: the President, together with his National Security Council; the Defense Department; and State (which now includes the Arms Control and Disarmament Agency). How closely and in what detail they really collaborate and coordinate only few people know. In my seven years' experience in the policy end of things in the Pentagon, I had two personal contacts with the State Department, one of which involved the Secretary, one with Alan Dulles, head of the CIA and one with McGeorge Bundy, the National Security Adviser. Only one of the contacts might be called a policy matter; I was asked to brief members of State on the war plan for Vietnam. It was a short meeting, apparently satisfying their need. To my knowledge there were few staff-to-staff meetings between the principal departments; there were ad hoc groups between State and Defense that popped up from time to time.

And note again that there is no record that the President's "National Security Strategy" (Chapter 6) was coordinated with the State Department/Arms Control Agency.

A New Course

Shifting gears now, I introduce a matter which gets to the heart of the job of the president's formulation and implementation of national security policy. In fact, the following contains not only a policy, with which I am generally in accord, but demonstrates how complicated the issues are; it sets the stage for a new way of managing the implementation of foreign policy, particularly when dealing with aggression in the world.

To begin, I draw on an article, "Charting a New Diplomatic Course: Alternative approaches to Post-Cold War Foreign Policy," by the Miller Center Journal, Miller Center of Public Affairs at University of Virginia, to address its formulation. And I see this piece as a significant improvement to the White House Policy. It is a stepping-stone on the way to my strategy. Although brief, it cites 92 "Endnotes" by famous and/or informed people, attesting to its thoroughness.

It starts, "The end of the Cold War has transformed the nature of the international system, presenting the United States with a long list of serious, novel, ongoing challenges in foreign affairs, and evoking a wide range of these orientations: historic and contemporary versions of isolationist thought, conservative neoisolationism, liberal neoisolationism, conservative interventionism, liberal interventionism, and the pragmatic interventionism approach to foreign policy." In my lingo, proponents of foreign policies have been all over the barn in their solutions. These authors chose the latter approach, pragmatic internationalism, with which I resonate the most.

They continue, "Combining the views of several advocates of this approach, it is possible to enumerate ten guidelines for a pragmatic interventionist approach to American foreign policy after the Cold War. (Underling supplied for emphasis).

"1. In any decision to commit American power abroad—especially its military power—the national interest should be clear and compelling. Any interventions must contribute directly and significantly to American security and well-being. The president and his advisers must clarify and articulate the national interest for the American people.

"2. There must be clear sense of mission whenever our nation's armed forces are committed overseas. The objectives of projecting American power abroad must initially be clear to policy makers in Washington, and in time to the American people. Policy makers must also avoid "mission creep," or changing the goals of military intervention after the armed forces have become engaged. These constraints are essential for setting any kind of timetable for withdrawing

US forces, <u>with broad international support for the venture,</u> and deciding whether the undertaking was ultimately successful.

"3. A pragmatically based diplomacy also requires officials in Washington to undertake a 'cost-benefit analysis' in formulating policy. Decision makers must objectively weigh the consequences of alternative courses of action. <u>The concept of costs must be broadly construed to include not only casualties and financial expenditures, but also the potential loss of goodwill among friends and allies, erosion of diplomatic credibility, and creation of deep political divisions at home.</u>

"4. Many pragmatists believe that, when crises erupt abroad, <u>other forms of power ought to be used before military force.</u> They think policy makers should reserve the nation's military power for times when other forms of power have failed to achieve the objective.

"5. <u>American power should be committed abroad only when it would make a permanent difference in shaping the outcome of events beyond America's borders.</u> This stipulation is a product of interventions in Lebanon, East Africa, Haiti and Bosnia. In several instances, US intervention not only failed to remove the underlying causes of political upheaval and conflict, but further complicated existing problems.

"6. Policymakers must make decisions with a sense of regional priorities. Throughout America's diplomatic history, some regimes have been more important to America's security and diplomatic interests than others. For example, ever since the Monroe Doctrine (1823), policymakers have insisted that peace and security in the Western Hemisphere is of vital diplomatic interest to the United States. Until World War ll, although many citizens did not appear to be aware of it, the nation's security depended on the European balance of power. In the twentieth century, America fought two wars to preserve the West's security. In 1949, NATO has been and remains the nation's most important alliance system. More recently, the Middle East has emerged as a vital American security zone. America's military security and economic prosperity continues to depend on the unimpeded access to the Persian Gulf's oil supplies.

"7. <u>The United States must make every effort to gain international support before intervening abroad.</u> This is one of the most important 'lessons of Vietnam.' <u>The Persian Gulf was a model of</u>

multinational cooperation in an interventionist undertaking. The wisdom and legitimacy of intervention fundamentally depends on allied support.

"8. Most pragmatists believe American military intervention should be limited. The power needed to achieve a diplomatic goal should not indefinitely drain national resources. American military intervention should also be limited in duration. There should also be a reasonably clear timetable for withdrawing US forces. Most fundamentally perhaps, the objectives of American intervention should be limited. Even in the militarily successful war in the Persian Gulf War, the United States and its allies pursued limited goals. They refrained, for example, from trying to change the nature of the Iraqi political system, or democratizing governments throughout the Middle East.

"9. Congress must support any US intervention for it to succeed. The legislative branch possesses certain important prerogatives and powers in the foreign policy field, such as determining the size and nature of the military establishment and for providing funds for a long list of international programs. Traditionally regarded as the voice of the people, Congress must provide tangible and intangible support for major diplomatic undertakings.

"10. Finally, any successful US intervention must have public support. It is axiomatic that, in a democratic system, the government's internal and external policies must have and retain 'the consent of the governed.'"

I add another, but all-important, guideline, The United States will conform with international law in any military operations and will operate through and/or coordinate with the UN Security Council in accordance the UN Charter.

The authors continue, "Admittedly, many citizens do not seem interested in international issues. Some people are content to follow the president's lead in dealing with external problems. At the very least, however, projecting the nations' power abroad must not elicit public opposition. On the contrary, for public support, intervention must be legitimate and must somehow promote American security and well-being."[1]

---

[1] Crabb, Serieddine and Antizzo, Miller Center Journal, Miller Center of Public Affairs, University of Virginia. Vol. 4, Spring 1997.

That term in paragraph 10, 'the consent of the governed,' is 'us.' We have an obligation to stay informed of the issues, which this book endeavors to do and, further, we must articulate our approval or disapproval of the manner and means of seeking foreign policy objectives, particularly when US military forces are involved. This book would seem to fall into this category.

More on Shaping Nations

National security has been discussed above and in Part 2, Chapters 6 and 8. Now a look at the way the US relates to other nations day-to-day.

An observer and professor of history for forty-five years, Professor, Emeritus, of History and Public Affairs, Norman Graebner, gave a talk, " The Limits of Meliorism in Foreign Affairs" at University of Virginia's Miller Center of Public Affairs in August, 1998 which illuminates recent and current foreign affairs (Several of his books are listed in the Acknowledgements.)

The word "meliorism" was new to me, so the dictionary cleared it up—almost. Its definition, "the belief that the world tends to get better and, especially, that this tendency can be furthered by human effort." After hearing the talk and mulling it over for a while, I came up with an adjunct definition, "Do good-ism, with an ironic twist." And after more thought, this old aphorism came to mind, "The road to Hell is paved with good intentions."

The following are excerpts and a condensation of his talk.

Graebner said that not since classic Rome did a single state tower so completely over its potential rivals. Mark Whittaker proclaimed in "Newsweek" that its true superpower status permitted the US no choice but to use force, both in its own defense and in the defense of international law and democratic values. Graebner went on, "Clearly such expressions of global obligations had no precedent in the county's history. William Clinton and his foreign policy team promised that after January 1993, US policy would again focus on expanding democracy and human values. There would, he promised, be interventions not only to defend national interests, but also for reason of national conscience."

And then there are the specific cases. In Haiti, Clinton maneuvered its leader out of office, in the process causing widespread starvation and a steady flow of refugees to the US. With new leadership, four years later, in 1998 Haiti was a basket case, politically, economically and socially.

While the US did take the initiative in the Dayton Accord, the occupying NATO forces, led by the US, achieved a peace, but failed to resettle the refugees, deserted the goal of a multi-ethnic state, and refused to pursue those guilty of genocide. NATO forces still remain there.

And now, the nations that defy the norms of behavior as defined and declared by the Defense Department: Cuba, North Korea, Iran, Iraq and Libya, labeled "rogue nations." Anthony Lake observed that the United States carried a special responsibility for developing a strategy to neutralize, contain and, through selective pressure, perhaps eventually transform these backlash states into constructive members of the international community. Graebner observed that such adverse judgments of other governments never contributed much to the resolution of international conflicts. They rationalized an unwillingness to examine the rejected country's outlook, motives, and objectives, none of which endangered US interests. He added that Washington's intention toward many of these countries included elimination of their leaders. And that the US officials could hardly negotiate successfully with governments that they hope to displace. He said, repeatedly the US inability to act lay in the formulation of objectives that were essentially unilateral, reached without consultation with others, but whose achievement required international cooperation.

Graebner points out that the Helms-Burton Act, which sought to undermine Castro completely by denying Cuba hard currency, embarked on a crusade to deprive Cuba of all foreign trade and investment. Europeans, Canadians and Latin Americans opposed it. Graebner said the effort failed totally. America's friends rejected the very idea of making foreign policy under the threat of a lawsuit. One Canadian official, he said, complained that America's domestic politics had crashed headlong into everybody else's foreign policy.

The UN General Assembly voted 183-3 for a resolution condemning the US economic embargo of Cuba.

Washington also took tough action against Libya and Iran by imposing sanctions, thereby restricting access to US markets and economic opportunities for foreign investments that were doing business with them, imperiling projects that had heavy French and Italian funding. The Atlantic Alliance threatened the strategic relationship between the US and its European partners by disrupting trade. The Canadian Prime Minister observed, "Unilateral application of international law is unacceptable." France's President Chirac warned, "The European Union will retaliate if the D'Amato bill [originated in the Senate by D'Amato] becomes law. And I do not want that off the record. In spite of the warnings President Clinton signed the bill on August 5, 1996."

Clearly the unilateralism and partisanship that sustained the country's long animosity toward Iran and Iraq scarcely serves the interests of the United States. Recall the CIA's role visa-a-vis Iraq.

Graebner goes on. "It was not strange the limited gains for democracy, peace and stability in the post-Cold War world led to a renewed call for the always-elusive American role in world affairs that reflect the country's superpower status. For some citizens, America's global role, its obligations and its security, continued to rest in a greater exertion of force than a more competent and determined effort to influence and shape the world's institutions. Meliorists presumed that the United States alone possessed the power, prestige, technology, wealth and virtue required to reform whole countries, if not the world. Clinton's record demonstrated that the United States had neither the knowledge nor the power to institute democracy and order in other lands.

Faced by a nationalistic and resistant world, pursuing its own interests and reflecting its own conditions, Clinton's meliorism, characterized by an arrogant, defiant unilateralism, not only failed, it denied the country the natural, realistic, unobtrusive, potentially stabilizing role that the deeply troubled world required."[2]

[2]From a talk given by Professor Norman Graebner titled, "The Limits of Meliorism in Foreign Affairs" at the University of Virginia Miller Center, August, 1998. See Acknowledgements.

Another observer of international affairs, George Melloan, makes the case that the United States is shooting from the hip, that it has no central core policy that steers all foreign policy and actions. He cites the way Saddam Hussein has been pulling the marionette strings.

Melloan starts, " Once again, for the second time in less than a year, Saddam Hussein has baited Bill Clinton into enormous commitment of wealth and manpower. Again, Saddam has backed down, leaving the American president helpless and frustrated. . . . Mr. Clinton for the second time in less than a year was forced to dispatch ships and planes to within striking distance of Iraq. . . . But Mr. Clinton doesn't have months to keep his planes and ships on station in a state of high alert. The cost could run into billions of dollars, more even than it did last winter. . . . So why did Mr. Clinton twice play into Saddam's hands? The answer is that Saddam has a better understanding than Bill Clinton himself of how the American president operates."[3]

We have just completed a look at what seems to me a clear and logical new policy (with my addition of paragraph 11). Editor in Chief of Air Force Magazine, John T. Correll's "Lessons in Limited Force," is an extension of pragmatic interventionism, amounting to a policy within a policy. He begins, "In one ambiguous operation after another, the Clinton Administration practically conducted a clinic in 1998 on the shortcomings of limited force. It must have set some sort of record for the variety and number of instances in which he used or threatened to use military force to send political signals, crack the whip on one recalcitrant foe, or pursue some other limited objective.

The administration came to office in 1993 believing that the policy for committing US forces to combat should be relaxed. Under the new policy, lethal military power could be used in small increments for limited purposes, even if no vital US interest was at stake or if our intentions were a little fuzzy. Such actions reached a peak in 1988.

---

[3]By George Melloan, "Another Defeat for Ad Hoc Foreign Policy," Wall Street Journal, November 17, 1998, Published by permission of Dow Jones, Inc. via Copyright Clearance Center, Inc. (C) 1999 Dow Jones and Company. All Rights Reserved Worldwide.

As the year began, the White House had maneuvered itself into a showdown with Iraq over weapons inspections. However, it was not prepared to follow through on its blustering threats of military force, UN Secretary Kofi Annan defused that crisis by brokering a deal in which we accepted transparently false promises from the Iraqi leader Saddam Hussein and rewarded him with concessions. In June, UN inspectors found the residue of nerve gas in an Iraqi weapons pit.

In August, Iraq refused to permit any more spot inspections. In public, we talked tough and issued more warnings. Privately, the State Department was pressuring the inspectors to ease up as we edged toward a less confrontational policy.

On August 20, US warships launched 79 cruise missiles against the terror network of Osama bin Laden . . . for the bombing of our embassies in Kenya and Tanzania. . . ."

The scene shifted again in October. After repeated threats and warnings throughout the summer—during which Serbian leader Slobodan Milosevic ran up the casualty count in Kosovo—the US and NATO allies planned airstrikes, postponed them, planned them again, and finally canceled them on Milosevic's pledge of good behavior. By December, with peace in Kosovo coming apart at the seams, the State Department was sending new and stronger warnings to Milosevic.

In late October, Iraq ended all cooperation with the UN inspectors. For once even eight Arab states blamed Saddam for the worsening crisis, but President Clinton could not bring himself to pull the trigger. On Nov. 14, with B-52 bombers already in the air, he aborted the strikes on the strength of an unseen letter from Saddam to Kofi Annan. Within hours, the White House discovered the letter had "more holes than Swiss cheese," rescheduled the airstrikes, then aborted them a second time when Saddam submitted a revised letter.

The provocations soon resume, and so did the warnings, On Dec. 16, acting on a UN inspector's report on Saddam defiance, the White House ordered Desert Fox to begin. There was less international support than for the aborted attack in November, and the visible provocation was no greater, but the Administration said the operation could not be delayed, even for a few days. It launched 650 air sorties and 400 cruise missiles against Iraq, but it had all the earmarks of a limited force.

The considerations in Desert Fox were mostly political rather than military. Avoidance of casualties—on the Iraqi side as well as our own—was a big constraint, as was concern about world opinion. Our objectives were stated in language of hesitation: to "degrade," "diminish," or "weaken" Saddam's position. There was no plan to "destabilize" the Iraqi dictator. . . .

Desert Fox was not a valid measure of military power. In a tactical sense, it could be judged a success. The four-day bombing campaign was effective against the assigned targets, but the strategic value of it was dubious. Saddam emerged from it with an enhanced standing in the international community. Within a week, Iraq . . . was shooting at American and British aircraft in the no-fly zone.

Iraqi Vice President Yassin Ramadan . . . told reporters last November that Iraq does not fear the threat of the United States because it has been threatening Iraq for the past eight years.

Going to war—or threatening to do so—is a serious step. Combat operations ought to be a last resort, undertaken only when other approaches fail and when we are grimly steadfast in our purpose.

In February 1998, though, described the potential action against Iraq that was roughly the same scope as Operation Desert Fox, Secretary of State Madeleine Albright said 'we are talking about using military force, but we are not talking about war.'

That distinction has not served us very well so far. Neither has the doctrine of Limited Force, with its legacy of half measures and lost credibility. The experience of 1998 strongly suggests that we should think again about the use of force and the thresh-hold of combat."[4]

Following on the heels of Editor Correll's critique of US policy we find that the US has engaged in deceitful actions with UNSCOM in Iraq. Barton Gellman's front page Washington Post article starts, "United States intelligence services infiltrated agents and espionage equipment for three years into United Nations arms

[4] Reprinted by permission from Air Force Magazine, February, 1999, Published by the Air Force Association.

control teams in Iraq to eavesdrop on the Iraqi military without the knowledge of the UN agency that it used to disguise its work. . . .

By all accounts the UN Special Commission, or UNSCOM, did not authorize or benefit from this channel of US surveillance. This contrasts with previous statements in which the Clinton Administration acknowledged use of eaves-dropping equipment but said it was done solely in cooperation with UNSCOM to pierce Iraqi conceal-ment of its illegal weapons . . . the United States rigged UNSCOM equipment and office space—without permission—to intercept a high volume of ordinary Iraqi military communications . . . between microwave towers and linking Iraqi commanders to infantry and ar-mored forces in the field . . . of considerable value to US military planners but generally unrelated to UNSCOM's weapons mandate.

US government officials said they considered the risk of dis-crediting an international arms control system by infiltrating if for their own eaves-dropping. They said the stakes were so high in the conflict with Iraq, and the probability of discovery so low, that the risks were worth the running. . . .

But unbeknownst to UNSCOM, the US signals that sensor tech-nicians who installed and maintained the system were intelligence operatives, and repeater stations they built had a covert capability. Hidden in their structure were antennas capable of intercepting mi-crowave transmissions, the US agents placed some of them near im-portant nodes of Iraqi military communications. . . .

Until late last week, the US government appeared to deny cate-gorically that it placed covert agents on the UNSCOM teams without UNSCOM's knowledge and consent. In a January 7 briefing for six invited newspaper and television reporters, a high-ranking US offi-cial said: 'We didn't put people on the UN teams to be agents of the United States. Everyone we put on UNSCOM worked for UNSCOM. They were part of UNSCOM, not reporting separately. But after-wards, of course, they were debriefed.

In interviews for this story, spokesmen for the CIA Pentagon, White House and State Department declined to repeat any categori-cal denials.

Privately, according to close associates, UNSCOM Chief But-ler expressed distress when he first learned of the allegations . . . saying 'If this stuff turns out to be true, then Rolf Ekeus and I have been played for suckers, haven't we? . . . I've spent a lifetime of helping to build and defend the nonproliferation regimes. Piggy-backing in this manner [by US intelligence] can only serve the in-terests of those who reject meaningful efforts at arms control."[5]

Next is an incisive article titled "Military Obsession," by Oscar Lurie, Associate Research Analyst at the Center for Defense Infor-mation, Washington DC.[6]

It sheds further light on how our government operates.

"America's decision-makers appear to be obsessed with a drive to expand our super-power military to hyper-power—status. While the hundreds of fighter planes in our inventory exceed the capabili-ties of any aircraft elsewhere in the world, we have scheduled the building of more than three thousand aircraft in three even more powerful designs. Our Navy, already able to deploy twelve of the world's most powerful aircraft carriers, has two more under construc-tion costing over $9 billion; it is also expanding its fleet of super-powerful nuclear submarines at a price exceeding $3 billion each.

Money is no object. The US by itself spends $281 billion on its military, more than the total spent by 25 of its closest allies and friends. Countries of most concern to the US—Russia, China, India and Pakistan (because of their recent nuclear and missile tests), and the seven "rogue states"—together spend less than half the US total on their military forces. Yet over the next six years, President Clin-ton wants to increase America's military spending by more than $110 billion—and Congress thinks even this insufficient!

What accounts for this profligate mind set? Several causes contribute:

- The pressure of defense contractors for more business and profits.

---

[5] By Barton Gellman, **Copyright 1999, The Washington Post, Reprinted with permission**

[6] Center for Defense Information, Weekly Defense Monitor, 2-4-99, articles by Oscar Lurie and Rachel Stohl. Email address: owner-weekly@mail.cdi.org

- The hunger of Congressman for jobs (and votes) in their home areas.
- The foreign policy lobbies in the media, academia, and private think tanks who must trumpet the need for large military forces to justify their own employment.

But by themselves these influences do not account for directing just over half of the federal government's discretionary (that is, non-mandatory) budget to the military. There is also an emotional predisposition toward powerful fighting forces and a tough foreign policy. In plain words this is an obsession to be "king of the hill." Opinion makers give this emotion an attractive, positive label—leadership. A more appropriate label is "domination."

The drive for domination produces some strange choices. While the Pentagon spends millions of dollars on 'force protection' for the military, the commission chaired by retired Admiral William Crowe found the provisions made for the security of US embassies and diplomats almost universally inadequate. The commission cited a collective failure of the US government over the past decade" to provide adequate protection for US personnel abroad. Among the other reasons for this failure is the cost of constructing redesigned facilities.

Although the Crowe commission was too polite to say so, diverting a few billion dollars from the defense budget to the basic security of our non-military overseas representatives might have dissuaded those who attacked our Nairobi and Dar Es Salaam embassies. Instead, America responded to the havoc wreaked on these two African embassies by pounding Afghanistan and Sudan with missiles that cost more than what should have been devoted to protecting these embassies.

The bombing of Iraq also illustrates this obsession with military action at the expense of political and diplomatic foreign policy avenues. The US called the bombing 'leading,' but only Britain followed. Russia and France [geographically much closer to Iraq than America] do not seem to believe that Saddam is a serious threat to international order. And Iraq's neighbors seem so little concerned that they are reluctant to provide basing for US forces.

Of all the emotions that underlie our policy-makers' obsession, threat-based concerns seem least important. Customarily, military buildups have been prompted by enemy threats. Yet our military planners now see so little threat to America that they downplay threats as the basis for force structure planning and substitute the concept of "capability." This is what drives the current acquisition of a cornucopia of weapons that, while technologically possible, are not the weapons that can best enable our armed forces to meet the real threats to our national security—including those that the Pentagon itself names.

There are other intangible factors which play a role in the current military spending binge:

- Pride and vanity: America won two world wars and beat the Soviets in the cold war. As the greatest economy in the world, we can afford to spend more of our resources on our military.
- Sheer enjoyment of a good a fight: mayhem football has replaced baseball as our national sport. Our movies and TV are full of violence and some of the actors are dressed in uniforms. All of us (except some mothers) enjoy them and give them high box office and Nielsen ratings.
- Suspicion and indifference: when a disgruntled American blew up the federal office building in Oklahoma City, the first reaction was to blame a foreign Arab conspiracy. Few Americans protest the US-led blockade of Iraq although we know it results in malnourishment and death for thousands of Iraqi children.
- A warped sense of "duty": our domineering policies induced friends and allies to reduce their military capabilities to the point they are unwilling to commit resources to help preserve peace in their own neighborhoods. By default, the US assumes the "moral" obligation to use our military when their peace is threatened. Hence the Dayton accord and American troops in Bosnia—on the doorstep of our western European friends.

These emotions engender a militarism that all too easily masquerades as an exaggerated and warped patriotism. Left free of rational control, human ingenuity will continue to develop and employ weapons of ever-increasing destructiveness. Instead of focusing energy on dominating the world military, the US should be exerting effort to lead in the diplomatic, economic, and where necessary the humanitarian arenas. And we should be devoting more talent and resources to creating the kind of international system that in the future will have the capability of effectively shouldering more of the burdens of keeping the world at peace."

   In the same Defense Monitor Analyst Rachel Stohl homes in on the world arms trade and the United States role in selling arms—still another role the US plays in the world.

"ACDA [Arms Control and Disarmament Agency] Releases Annual Arms Transfer Report

   "At the end of January the U.S. Arms Control and Disarmament Agency finally released via the Internet the first part of its annual report," 'World Military Expenditures and Arms Transfers 1997' or WMEAT. The report, which had been expected last summer, contains data on world-wide arms transfers for 1996.

   Noteworthy in this latest edition is a recalculated data formula that gives a more representative picture of U.S. arms sales. The revision concerns the commercial component of U.S. arm sales, those between U.S. firms and foreign importers that are licensed through the Department of State. The revision does not affect arms exports under the Department of Defense's Foreign Military Sales (FMS) program. Under the recalculated data, commercial exports totaled 52 percent of all U.S. arms exports, FMS sales 47 percent, and other smaller export programs the remaining one percent. Using the new methodology, the dollar value of direct commercial sales grew from $1.1 billion to 10.6 billion of total U.S. exports.

   However, the new methodology represents only a quick fix to a larger problem: the lack of reliable data on commercial arms exports. The explanation of the changes provided in the WMEAT—Revision of U.S. Arms Export Data Series—says that pending the establishment of reliable recording of actual commercial exports, the U.S. arms exports data series in this edition of WMEAT incorporates an estimated data series employing an interim methodology, which is to be replaced in an early successor edition with a more satisfactory solution based on ongoing research efforts.

   Even if this year's report uses an 'estimated data series employing an interim methodology,' the revision had a significant impact on the reported values of U.S. arms exports. For the 1986-96 decade, arms sales are 45 percent higher on average and for 1990-96 60 percent higher.

WMEAT reported that the world arms trade in 1996 was $42.7 billion, an increase of $2 billion from the 1995 report. The rise was attributed to a $3 billion increase in imports by the developed world that was only partially offset by a $1 billion decrease in the developing world. The report also found that the U.S. primarily supplies weapons to developed countries. In 1996, U.S. exports to the developed world were 33 percent of world trade and 61 percent of total U.S. arms exports. According to these figures, the developed world received 75 percent of its total arms imports from the U.S. Conversely, in the same period, the developing world received 61 percent of their arms transfers from non-U.S. sources and only 39 percent from U.S. suppliers—still the largest single exporter to the developing world.

According to the WMEAT publication, the top ten arms exporters in 1996 controlled 94 percent of the world trade. The top ten are:

Country	Billions U.S.$	Percent of Total
United States	23.50	55
United Kingdom	6.10	14
Russia	3.30	8
France	3.20	8
Sweden	1.20	3
Germany	.83	2
Israel	.68	2
China	.60	1
Canada	.46	1
Netherlands	.34	<1

In terms of exports to the developing world, WMEAT reported the following top exporters:

Country	Billions U.S.$	Percent of Total
United States	9.2	39
United Kingdom	5.6	24
Russia	2.8	12
France	2.1	9
China	.6	3
Israel	.4	2
Canada	.2	1

ACDA's data showed that three regions of the world were responsible for 80 percent of total world arms imports in 1996. These regions were the Middle East with 38 percent, East Asia with 22 percent, and Western Europe with 21 percent. WMEAT 's top ten importing countries, responsible for 57 percent of all arms imports in 1996, are:

Country	Billions U.S.$	Percent of Total
Saudi Arabia	9.8	23
Japan	2.4	6
Taiwan	2.0	5
Egypt	1.8	4
Kuwait	1.7	4
China	1.5	4
United Kingdom	1.5	4
Turkey	1.4	3
Australia	1.3	3
South Korea	1.1	3

ACDA's [Arms Control and Disarmament Agency] development of a new and more accurate methodology is welcome. The reports' authors also recognize that there are still significant problems with the calculations, saying that there are significant problems in tracking direct commercial sales. However, the WMEAT's utility is open to question because the data is so dated. Other government publications, such as the Congressional Research Service's report on U.S. arms exports to the developing world, have more recent data available for analysis. This dichotomy fuels the frustration felt by many researchers since the U.S. is one of the world's most transparent countries with respect to publishing arms trade data."[6]

Managing the Executive Branch

After an insight into the complexity of determining foreign policy; now comes the matter of managing foreign affairs in all its aspects. Yes, our president has the unenviable task of heading the management, not only of policy formulation but its execution, and doing all the concrete actions, and their coordination.

We have a good example of how it should not be done; back to Robert McNamara's critique of the Vietnam War, his eleventh and last point in his book deals with the issue of management:

"11. Underlying many of these errors lay our failure to organize the top echelons of the executive branch to deal effectively with the extraordinary complex range of political and military issues, involving the great risks and costs—including, above all else, loss of life—associated with the application of military force under substantial constraints over a long period of time. Such organizational weakness would have been costly had this been the only task confronting the president and his advisers. It, of course, was not. It co-existed with the wide array of other domestic and international problems confronting us. Thus we failed to analyze and debate our actions in Southeast Asia—our objectives, the risks and the costs of alternative ways of dealing with them, and the necessity of changing course when failure was clear—with the intensity and thoroughness that characterized the debates of the Executive Committee during the Cuban Missile crisis."

My solution: the establishment of a permanent coordination group, entitled 'The Operations Coordination Group', for want of a better name. Its role: assure the coordination of not only the establishment of policy but the myriad day-to-day operations of all facets of implementing national security. The thesis of this book will require considerable more attention and action involving the countless new facets of peacemaking, peacekeeping, disarmament and prevention, which should be pursued with at least the same priority as managing war and its preparation. Said another way, shifting to a policy of Rule of Law will require countless changes in every area of government, requiring special management and coordination, and requiring a new modus operandi, such as the Operations Coordination Group.

Its composition: senior individuals seconded to the heads of the National Security Council, the White House staff, State/Arms Control and Disarmament Agency, Defense, CIA and the Atomic Energy Commission. The State member would be the appropriate head of the unit. Its functions: assure coordination and facilitate all facets of the implementation, primarily of the White House, State and Defense, of foreign and military policies; keep their superiors informed; brief the President and the National Security Council and each other, in normal times as well as in crises. Particularly important is the coordination of policy making as well as its execution of the State's arms control and preventive measures with Defense's weapons development and the testing of new weapons. A case in point, the issue of the need of a missile defense. The purpose: preventing another arms race. This mechanism would provide more assurance that all principals are fully informed, and that the process is working smoothly, especially in fast-breaking national security matters. Its principal members would be present at decision-making meetings on relevant issues. The department heads would continue to perform their normal duties. This structure should keep the President fully informed, cope with the myriad of the fast moving events, and permit all the department heads to perform their routine business more effectively.

The White House National Security Council has the most onerous task of all: providing sound policy advice to the President.

20

Fixing the Security Council

First, the Veto

I've said a number of times that altering the power of the 15 member Security Council is important. Now I say that most important of all is the veto power of the five Permanent Members. Yes, crucial.

It was the veto or the threat of a veto by a Permanent Member that tied the hands of the Security Council during the forty-odd years of the Cold War. Now, in this relatively benign period, is the opportunity to prevent the abuse of the veto.

A Permanent Member should not have the right to prevent the Security Council from carrying out its primary function of maintaining the peace through implementation of Rule of Law; any Permanent Member of the Security Council which is a party to an issue under consideration should, in all fairness, recuse—refrain—from voting, just as judges everywhere must do when impartial judgment does not seem possible. Employing such objectivity would gain enormous respect for the Permanent Five and allay legitimate concerns of the smaller nations. There is no *obligation* to vote or exercise a veto; nations can, and often have, refrained voluntarily from doing so.

What's vitally needed in addition, though, is a means to assure impartial 'judges.' No Perm Five Member should be allowed to be, simultaneously, an accused and a 'judge' of the legality of its own behavior. Specifically, when a vetoing Perm Five Member is deemed by majority vote of the Security Council to be, for instance, in violation of international law or the UN Charter. Examples of violations of international law or the UN Charter include: the crime of aggression or a party thereto; providing other nations with illicit weapons, such as chemical, biological or (eventually) nuclear weapons, or the means to create such illicit weapons outlawed by binding treaties; or to deliver them, e.g., by missile.

One method is for the Security Council to adopt a procedural rule which would prevent such misuse of power by a Perm Five Member. It would be a mockery if a Big Five rogue was able to block—veto—the violations listed above. In this connection the Charter provides (Article 30), that "The Security Council shall adopt its own rules of procedure, including the method of selecting its President." Article 27 provides that "Decisions of the Security Council on procedural matters shall be made by an affirmative vote of nine members" and, "Decisions of the Security Council on all other matters shall be made by an affirmative vote of nine members including the votes of the permanent members" in certain matters in which "a party to a dispute shall abstain from voting." Extending the interpretation of Article 27 to the vitally important violations cited above would make the difference between war and peace, or perpetuating a rogue Permanent Member—as was the case in the Cold War.

I offer an alternate approach: threaten to start proceedings to expel a rogue Permanent Five Member or, if necessary, proceed to do so.

Nations which persistently violated the principles contained in the Charter may be expelled from the Organization by the General Assembly upon recommendation of the Security Council.

Within the above Charter provisions there is plenty of leverage to make a rogue Member of the Security Council comply. In this connection, Chapter 1, Article 2 of the UN Charter provides:

> "2. All Members, in order to ensure to all of them the rights and benefits resulting from membership, shall fulfill in good faith the obligations assumed by them in accordance with the present Charter.
>
> 3. All Members shall settle their international disputes by peaceful means in such a manner that international peace and security, and justice, are not endangered.
>
> 4. All members shall refrain in their international relations from the threat or use of force against a territorial integrity or political independence of any state, or in any other manner inconsistent with the purposes of the United Nations.

5. All members shall give the United Nations every assistance in any action it takes in accordance with the present Charter, and shall refrain from giving assistance to any state against which the United Nations is taking preventive or enforcement action."

Chapter II, Membership, provides:

4. Membership in the United Nations is open to all peace loving states which accept the obligations contained in the present Charter and in the judgment of the Organization are able and willing to carry out these obligations.

5. A Member of the United Nations against which preventive and enforcement action has been taken by the Security Council may be suspended from the exercise of rights and privileges of membership by the General Assembly upon recommendation of the Security Council. The exercise of these rights and privileges may be restored by the Security Council.

6. A Member of the United Nations which has persistently violated the principles contained in the present Charter may be expelled from the Organization by the General Assembly upon recommendation of the Security Council."

If worldwide Rule of Law is ever to be realized, hardball methods, such as compliance or expulsion or the threat thereof, will be needed to quell outlaws. At the ultimate, though, a Security Council Member, including a Permanent Member, could decide to resign from the United Nations over a crucial issue. Better that than one nation nullifying or forestalling the Security Council on a crucial issue, such as the forty-odd years of blocking the will of the Security Council by the Soviet Union during the Cold War. Should the rogue nation resign, it could find itself at odds with the entire world, and an array of impediments in its path. A dire decision.

Worldwide Rule of Law is on the line. It's either worldwide Rule of Law, with its means of enforcement, or we continue in the jungle. It will take a strong nation to lead the way forward. The only viable candidate—the United States. We have the potential, and the military might, but our might must be channeled wholly into enforcing Rule of Law. Are we up to the task, to shoulder this momentous responsibility?

Upon the publication of this book, I will provide a copy to each member of the Security Council.

Instituting these processes will cause a profound change for the better in the way nations relate to each other. *Creating procedures whereby an unlawful veto could be voided is the most important procedure the Security Council can ever take.* No doubt nations, including the United States, would balk initially at giving up their accustomed freedom of action. (The sorts of activities the United States would, no doubt, have to forego are discussed in Chapter 18, Part II of the book). But reflection will show that international law would be the winner, war the loser.

Creating it or not could well determine whether there will be another World War one day—as well as lesser aggressions and violence. Countless lives and untold treasure are at stake. At issue is the ability of the Security Council to carry out the very heart and core of the fundamental purpose of the UN. It will either watch helplessly as wars start and end—or carry the day by preventing or defeating them with the proposed processes and through implementation of Rule of Law.

Just establishing the processes can act as a powerful incentive for Big Five Members—and all other nations—to adhere strictly to international law and, as well, be the primary promulgators of it.

Create The Combined Military Staff

A high priority is the provision of a competent, full-blown combined military staff. The Security Council's originally authorized Military Staff Committee (MSC), made up of the Permanent Five senior military officers, has not been utilized—after fifty-two years (I would propose that it be renamed the Combined Military Staff, as "Committee" is a very unmilitary title.) Not having a military staff for advice and planning is like the United States trying to operate without the Pentagon. This prominent lack showed in Somalia and early in Bosnia (until there was an agreed peace plan and a clear chain of command under NATO). What's needed is a full staff capable of planning the employment of quick reaction and stand-by forces to deal with the many situations which are bound to develop. Each situation will require its own mix and level of forces. There are no "one-suit-fits-all" situations. Because of the prodigious details, anticipation, and preplanning are essential. This is not the only method available to the Security Council. Individual nations could prepare multilateral plans. For the life of the UN, the Security Council has dealt at the strategic level with major violations of international law, starting with its role in the Korean War and more recently with the Gulf War, and with acts, such as Saddam Hussein's fuss over the UN inspection of possible weapons of mass destruction.

New Security Council Flexibility

The Security Council presently has available several methods open to it to effect military peacemaking operations, and together with already authorized Charter sanctions, embargoes and blockades, for dealing with rogues. The ways in which the Security Council can operate include:

1. Authorize the execution of an already unilaterally-planned military operation, as was done in the Gulf War, or
2. Designate a nation to create a multilateral plan for dealing with a rogue nation, or
3. Planning by the Security Council's Combined Military Staff, in conjunction with participating nations, or
4. Planning for the use of an available quick-reaction UN Peace Force to meet unforeseen contingencies in one or more of the several modes above.
5. Delegate authority to regional agencies.
6. When the staff is in place, plan and execute peacekeeping military operations (see below).

In all of the above, the required agreements with each nation and the Security Council would include safeguards to comply with a nation's constitutional requirements to declare war (much like NATO's Article V provision) and would provide that a nation need not agree to participate in a planned action until satisfied with the command and control arrangements. Note that President Bush offered Ft. Dix as the site for the Security Council military staff and training activities.

The Security Council, by directing publicly that planning be started for military action against a rogue nation, would send the message that it is the world vs. the rogue—a powerful deterrent. Had Saddam Hussein known that such a fate would befall him, it is unlikely that he would have undertaken his aggression into Kuwait. It is interesting to surmise whether WW II would actually have occurred had there been an effective, in-being UN Peace Force to deal with Japan's incursion into Manchuria and Hitler's tentative, tiny foray into the Rhineland. Certainly, history would have been far different. Once this technique becomes the norm, nations will have little reason to acquire weapons in excess of perceived defense needs, and then, in time, even these should dwindle. Just think of the resulting benefits. Astounding! All that's needed: global thinking, Rule of Law—instead of me, my, and mine.

Benjamin Ferencz, noted international lawyer who was a Chief Prosecutor for the United States for the Nuremberg trials (see Aknowledgements) wrote, "New Legal Foundations for Global Survival." In it he articulates in great detail the steps necessary to "save succeeding generations from the scourge of war." He states, "In sum, what is wrong with the current UN peacekeeping [I add, peacemaking as well] is that it underestimates its own authority, fails to uphold the Charter plan, does not know the size or nature of military forces required or available, covers a wide diversity of unrelated and uncoordinated obligations, has no comprehensive plan, lacks adequate or assured funding and needs professional planners and executors. What is required is a new organ of the Security Council that can handle all peace-maintenance problems in an orderly, planned, dispassionate and professional way—free of the shackles of national and regional or UN politics."

In addition to my proposals, he offers "Twelve Security Council Resolutions for Peace," covering legal obligations, judicial organs and enforcement. For the student of these issues, his book is a must.[1]

---

[1] Ben Ferencz, author of "New Legal Foundations for Global Survival," published by Oceana Publications, Dobbs Ferry, NY, 1994.

Peacekeeping

Peacekeeping, that is coping with lesser conflicts mainly internal to nations, has evolved upon the UN Secretary General and his staff by default—as member nations have not seen fit to provide the Charter authorized Military Staff Committee/Combined Military Staff, or the kind of staff that is actually required for both peace-making and peacekeeping. As a result of this void, hundreds of peacekeeping actions have fallen in the Secretary-General's lap, taking up an inordinate amount of the Secretary-General's time. It's like the Chairman of the Board of General Motors having to solve glitches in the production line or decide what should be done about the faulty air conditioning system. A case in point is the action in the Congo in 1960. The Secretary-General spent many a day and night having, personally, to determine not only policy but execution, too. The mode of organizing and implementing Peacekeeping operations remains virtually unchanged today. The Secretary-General must be the busiest, most overworked executive on earth.

Former Ambassador to the United Nations, Madeleine Albright, has proposed changes at the top echelons of the UN structure to help alleviate this situation. In this connection she said, "There is, after all, no more immediate or local an issue that whether our sons and daughters will some day be called upon to do battle in big wars because we failed to prevent or contain small ones." Major General Indar Rikhye, Indian Army, retired, who was the advisor to the Secretary-General on peacemaking, lays out in detail the required peacekeeping changes in his book, The Politics and Practice of UN Peacekeeping.[2]

Many fault the Secretary-General, but the member states have literally forced him by default into his back-breaking as well as near-impossible situation. Having to operate without adequate funds is only one factor. I refer to the US dues, in arrears to the tune of almost $1 billion or near 50% of the annual peacekeeping budget. But just as onerous is the lack of the Military Staff. I find it grossly unfair to criticize the Secretary-General when funds are withheld and when

---

[2] "The Politics and Practice of UN Peacekeeping—Past, Present and Future," by General Indar Rikhye.

vital military staff to do the work have not been provided. A rough analogy is shorting the US Secretary of Defense fifty percent of his operating funds while chopping out the Joint Chiefs of Staff and a large slice of the personnel in the Pentagon.

As the new Combined Military Staff becomes fully effective the Secretary-General can transfer most of his peacekeeping activities to the Security Council, keeping control of the political aspects.

As an aside, peacemaking—repelling aggression—is, in a way, easier to plan and execute than peacekeeping. Once the Security Council resolves to act, the primary role is handed over to a military commander to carry out his assigned mission. The Gulf War is an example of this. But peacekeeping operations have a far greater political input from beginning to end. Thus, far closer coordination between the new Combined Military Staff and the Secretary-General's staff will be required throughout operations.

Peacekeeping has become more complex with the passage of time and is now being categorized as: traditional preventive peace operations; peace enforcement; low-intensity peace operations in internal conflicts; humanitarian assistance; and, post-conflict peace building.

A primary pressing need are United Nations Charter-authorized regional agencies located in strategic areas. In view of the myriad of disputes in Africa a logical first choice would be there. On September 28, 1996, the Clinton Administration announced its initiative to organize and train an African peacekeeping force of 5,000 to 10,000 for use on the continent.

Note that while the US has shorted the UN on peacekeeping by $1 billion (50% of the annual peacekeeping budget) while at the same time it contributes only a tiny portion of Americans serving in these operations—627—and that the number of Americans serving has dropped five-fold since 1993.

Command and Control of Forces

Command and control arrangements for UN operations are rightfully sensitive and have been a major "stick point," notably in the Congress. No nation wants its troops squandered because of faulty planning or execution of operations. A solution lies in using tried techniques. Variations of NATO's structure, well known by four of the five Permanent Members, fill the bill. Security Council planning would provide that in large operations a political council of all involved nations be established to carry out its resolutions, implemented, in turn, by a supreme military commander (NATO has two). The United States would likely be asked to provide the senior commander in any such new situation.

Many do not have a clear understanding of command and control. American forces are always under the command of the President of the United States. In certain situations, however, US forces are "chopped" to the operational control of another commander, e.g. in NATO certain US divisions chop to the operational control of a German general upon execution of the NATO war plan. The US has been content with this arrangement since the beginning of NATO, over fifty years now. In the Gulf War several nations operated well under US operational control. Other control techniques: a coordinating authority (useful in coordinating strikes in multilateral offensive air operations, for example, for efficiency and safety), and assignment of geographic sectors of responsibility, as in WW ll in Europe and, currently, in Bosnia.

In my 1988 book, looking forward to the day when nuclear weapons were finally eliminated, I visualized this role for the Security Council: twenty ships painted white, an ICBM aboard, the UN insignia displayed, manned with international crews, several plying random courses worldwide continuously—to deter use of any nuclear weapons hidden by rogue nations.

In time, when weapons reductions and preventive measures are well under way and all the changes discussed here are instituted and in place, conventional weapons would be the remaining threat, with the threat to the United States, virtually nil.

Sovereignty

Sovereignty is an issue. Many fear loss of freedom of action. However, the United States has entered into numerous treaties, conventions and pacts, all limiting its sovereignty in some way—to achieve more important benefits. Even joining the UN involved some loss of sovereignty. Note that treaties are ratified by the US, with the advice and consent of the Senate. For example, under the two START pacts between the United States and Russia, nuclear weapons are being reduced mutually, thus limiting our capability. The key point is that the decisions were made because both sides gained. Looking at it differently, what kind of a world would it be if all nations insisted on 100% sovereignty? It's simply not possible. My favorite illustration of the benefits of international cooperation is that of the International Civil Aviation Organization, ICAO, the international body which regulates airline operations worldwide. Visualize a world without ICAO in which pilots select their own routes, choose their own altitudes, land whichever direction and speak whatever language. Pure chaos.

Recall my earlier dissertation on the President's, "A National Security Strategy for the New Century" and the "Quadrennial Defense Review" with respect to the matter of, "The US military plays an essential role in building coalitions and shaping the international environment in ways that protect and promote US interests." The Security Council has the potential of being the prime forum for shaping the international environment. There, the ego would have to be placed in a pocket. To attempt major military operations unilaterally perpetuates the old 'us' vs. 'them,' the age-old law of the jungle routine, along with their excessive costs. It would attract some friends, but tick off others and also spawn enemies of the US—instead of implementing Rule of Law. No nation can always have its will in the world. Agreements require compromise between nations, just as between the parties in our Congress. The Security Council is the forum in which the US should take the lead in shaping the international environment, and the lead in enforcing international law militarily.

With the military staff in place the execution of peacekeeping operations, too, should improve markedly. There is no question that US forces should continue to be topnotch. As a world leader, the US should initiate talks with all capable nations to line up forces for the UN Peace Force, as well as for peacekeeping.

As indicated in Chapter 3, the United States should start promoting negotiations, beginning with the Permanent Five nations to: eliminate all nuclear weapons; other existing mass destruction weapons; concepts for weapons of mass destruction; ICBMs; ICBM defense systems; and, also, tighten the Space Treaty to prohibit any weapons in space. Negotiations in this forum might speed up the consummation of these key agreements which have taken decades to complete. With the history of this century fresh in our mind, all nations having nuclear weapons and the capacity to make other mass destruction weapons—as well as all other nations—should welcome the opportunity to shed or avoid the burden of building these weapons, while at the same time increasing their security—provided that there is satisfactory inspection and verification. An expanded and restructured UNSCOM, which has done a commendable job dealing with weapons of mass destruction in Iraq, would be an appropriate body to take on the verification job. A refusal to permit inspectors to enter or to provide information could be answered by sanctions, embargo and blockade, already provided in international law, plus the Peace Force.

The strategic plan as outlined here has the potential for profound constructive change in the world through implementation of Rule of Law. The alternatives are clear. If we do not proceed, the mistakes of history will likely be repeated. This strategy costs virtually nothing to implement yet offers monumental savings of all kinds. My friend and severest critic, a local lawyer, says simply, "It won't work." My response to him, "Neither of us knows how well it will work—or even if it will work—but we must try, try to replace the turmoil and chaos of the 20th Century. What is your strategy for America?"

At best it will take time to solve the myriad other problems of lesser import for the United Nations to solve. The UN is not as efficient as we would wish but we tend to overlook our own many lapses and missteps, such as the Savings and Loan fiasco, the onerous $3.7 trillion national debt hanging over us, eliminating political campaign financing ills, the fact that the Department of Defense reportedly has lost control of its accounting, fixing social security, the weekly news reports on government waste, Vietnam, etc.—all this, and more, despite having the finest political institutions on earth.

21

What Do Americans Want?

As we now know, unless the American people support major military endeavors they are destined to fail, with the Vietnam War as a prime example. In the case of the New Strategy for America we know in advance what the American people want and don't want. Should this book send a clear message, and should the American people learn that there are feasible ways to achieve what they have been asking for, Katy bar the door. They will be beating at the door of the Congress and the White House for change!

Yes, the issues in the New Strategy for America herein outlined are infinitely important to America and Americans. Most every element of the New Strategy for America is supported in polls taken in recent years. The presidential candidates, however, have turned Americans' attention inward, centering their attention on domestic affairs: the economy, jobs, taxes, social security. In the last presidential campaign foreign affairs and national security were virtually nonexistent.

1. In the Americans Talk Issues Foundation polls taken in 1995:
   - 68 percent want the United States to pull back from its sole superpower role and let the rest of the world bear more of the burden.
   - 88 percent support UN standby forces.
   - 73 percent believe the UN should take the lead in stopping aggression.
   - 60 percent want nuclear weapons eliminated, by balanced and verifiable agreements.
   - 94 percent do not favor the notion of the United States fighting two wars simultaneously and doing it unilaterally.

- 68 percent favor monitoring as well as taxing international arms sales.[1]

2. Project on Peacekeeping & the United Nations reported in 1995:
   - 84% believe strengthening the UN is an "important" foreign policy goal for the United States; 51% view it as "very important." (Gallup 84% of Americans "strongly favor" the idea of UN peacekeeping operations. February 1994 poll by PIPA: Program on International Policy Attitudes, U. of Maryland School of Public Affairs).
   - 56% favor allowing US troops to serve under UN command under some circumstances. (L.A. Times poll, January, 1995)

   Abolition 2000: a Survey on Nuclear Weapons, April 1, 1997 reports:
   - Elimination of nuclear weapons
     64% strongly favor
     13% somewhat favor
     21% oppose, strongly oppose or don't know
   - Do you feel safer knowing that the US and other countries have nuclear weapons, or would you feel safer if you knew for sure that no country including the US had nuclear weapons?
     12% feel safer with
     84% feel safer without
     4% don't know
   - When you think of Russia today, do you consider Russia to be an enemy or an ally of the United States?
     23% enemy
     47% ally
     5% both
     25% balance

[1] Americans Talk Issues, Suite 1120, 1511 K Street, NW Washington, DC. 20005.

- The United States has negotiated and signed agreements to eliminate biological and chemical weapons. Do you strongly agree, somewhat disagree or strongly disagree the US should negotiate an agreement to eliminate nuclear weapons?

   68% strongly agree

   19% agree

   13% other[2]

3. • Americans' opinions of the United Nations, September, 1997 :

   72% favorable or mostly favorable.

- As to world leadership:

   73% favored a shared leadership vs. 12% opting for single leadership.

- As to strengthening the UN as a priority:

   30% top priority, 53% some priority, 14% no priority.

- Should the US cooperate with the UN?

   59% agree, 30% disagree.

- As the US is the most powerful nation, should the US go its own way in international matters?

   62% disagree, 32% agree[3]

Take note that the above percentages translate to the positive desires of 133–184 million Americans of voting age.

Note: Some of the above have been abbreviated in the interest of clarity and conserving space.

[2] Provided by GRACE, Global Resource Action Center for the Environment, Survey by Lake, Snell, Perry & Associates, 1730 Rhode Island Ave. NW, Washington, DC Suite 400. Phone 202 776 9066.

[3] Poll by the Council for A Livable World Education Fund, 110 Maryland Ave., NE, Washington, DC, 20002. Phone, 202 546 7950.

22

The New Strategy for America

The President of the United States will be delivering a talk in just a few moments, Peter Jennings said. We have not been informed as to the subject, only that his aides say it is a speech of vital importance to the American people—and to people everywhere. To say the least, speculation has been high these last three days in anticipation. His audience is expected to be extraordinarily large due to the unusual way it's been handled.

And here he is . . . the President of the United States.

Good evening fellow Americans. As to the mystery surrounding my talk, I purposely asked that the subject be withheld. For some time I have been conferring with key members of the government on developing A New Strategy for America: the Secretaries of State and Defense, the Joint Chiefs of Staff as well as senior retired generals and admirals, the Director of the CIA, with my National Security Adviser and key members of the Congress. Former key officials in government of both parties contributed also. It is called the New Millennium Panel.

Before going any further, I wish to thank the American people for placing me in the Office of the President of the United States. I will do my utmost to meet your expectations—with which I wholly agree. While campaigning I was well aware of the significant majority of Americans who responded to my platform of a new strategy for America, who think deeply about the many changes needed to create a safer, saner world. My strategy is fully in accord with the vast majority of Americans, as reflected in the polls. Bringing it about will be my highest priority. Your continued support will be essential. All know my record and my view that our major police actions last century were far from optimum, that the assumption of the role of world policeman is, likewise, less than optimum. Also, you are aware that I viewed America's arms race with the Soviets as a lose-lose situation, and that I did the utmost in my power to bring it to an early end. Too, that I believe there are far better ways to deal with aggression, that much more can be done in the way of preventing the use of force. Yes, it is infinitely better to prevent wars than fight them.

This new national security strategy for the United States is a new departure that is designed to bring about a dramatic and fundamental change in the way nations have related to each other throughout the centuries. Some of the essential changes can be made by the United States, but others must be made in concert with other nations; I am confident that most will join in bringing them about, as they, too, will benefit.

The march of events convinced me that such change is essential. Nations—just as prehistoric tribes—have used every stratagem imaginable over the years to control, overrun, or conquer their neighbors. In the 20th century alone there were over 250 wars in which 110,000,000 people worldwide were killed; countless millions more were wounded, made homeless or bereaved.

The 20th Century was the bloodiest ever—six times bloodier than the last. In the five major wars in which the United States was involved this century 620,000 Americans in uniform were killed, and 1,131,000 wounded. The last century, from our first war to the last, we were at war almost two days every week on average.

A repetition of another world war cannot be permitted, nor its toll repeated; United States battle deaths in World War II were near 300,000, nearly 16,000,000 served, its costs over $4 trillion in current dollars. Korea and Vietnam's toll of American lives was close to 100,000, their costs exceeded $1 trillion. The Cold War alone cost over $13 trillion, the diversion of resources from constructive endeavors to war incalculable, and, to repeat, the record of our police actions this century, less than optimal.

Our $5.5 trillion dollar debt was amassed mainly through wars and arms races. Now, down to $3.7 trillion, it represents 45 percent of our entire annual gross national product.

The last century's record must not be repeated in the 21st Century.

The New Millennium Panel conducted a detailed analysis of our three police actions and other wars last century, concluding that we failed—sometimes badly—to assess properly not only the enemy but our allies, by ignoring the cultures of friends and the enemies alike, by not drawing in the Congress and the American people, by settling for cosmetic military help from allies rather than creating a genuine multilateral force; and, that by accepting dollars from allies in lieu of military assistance in the Gulf War, we placed our fighting men and women in the position of being mercenaries—or hired guns. The New Millennium Panel, using a scale of 0 to 10, arrived at a rating of 5.5, by assessing the mission undertaken in our three police action vs. the accomplishments or, in other words, an effectiveness rating of 55 percent. They made a special point to me of the fact that virtually all of the negative factors lay at the feet of our national leaders and that, in general, those in uniform performed brilliantly within the restraints imposed upon them.

In view of this unsatisfactory record I am convinced it's finally time that the age-old ways of the jungle are left behind. Now is the time to take a new path in this increasingly dangerous world. Science has advanced to the point where nations can be obliterated, where the entire earth can be made barren. Even more efficient, more destructive weapons now on the drawing boards are on the horizon; these, and the proliferation of in-being weapons of mass destruction will trigger arms races unless concerted prevention measures are taken. Space is rapidly becoming the newest battlefield. I will be speaking about these and the many other elements that make up The New Strategy for America.

Rule of Law has served our nation well. The Constitution that our forefathers bequeathed us is the key element in the success we Americans have enjoyed. I firmly believe that now is the time to institute Rule of Law worldwide. My short definition of world Rule of Law: nations living in harmony under international law, with mechanisms for dealing with nations which violate the law—just as individuals in our nation.

Rule of Law is what the founders of the United Nations had in mind for all nations, now supported by 185 nations. I see bringing the provisions of the UN Charter into full fruition as the most important step that can be taken at this point in history. This, together with effective means of enforcement, will change nations' current relationships to a totally new way of relating to each another—from the current 'one nation' vs. 'another,' or 'us' vs. 'them,' to the new 'law abiding' vs. 'outlaw,' where security and other international issues are consistently addressed, and international courts adjudicate differences—a truly profound change.

Yes, the United Nations has been in existence for more than fifty years, but has not yet received the support necessary to carry out fully the Charter's provisions, to reach its potential, its founders' vision—fundamentally, to maintain international peace and security; to take collective measures for the protection and removal of threats to the peace; for suppressing acts of aggression; to bring about by peaceful means and in conformity with the principles of justice and international law, settlements of international disputes which might lead to the breach of peace; and to achieve cooperation in solving international problems. Members agree to refrain from the threat of use of force against the territorial integrity or political independence of any state. In no way am I suggesting a world government.

I note with pride that it was Americans who played a central role in bringing the lofty vision of the United Nations into being.

I will now outline a series of actions which I'll be initiating in the near term. The eon-old practice of aggression must be stopped. History shows that frequently aggression starts with a small incursion, as Japan's in Manchuria and Hitler's in the Rhineland, leading to World War II. I see the primary function of United Nations as deterring aggression, but in its event, to quell it multilaterally, to nip it in the bud. Unfortunately, throughout the Cold War and its arms race, the former Soviet Union's use of the veto—or the threat to do so—stymied action by the Security Council, nullifying its effectiveness. And there are other vital functions of the Security Council which must not be frustrated.

Of critical importance in maintaining international peace and security—the Security Council's primary mission—is a solution to the misuse of the veto power of Permanent Five Members, which can be accomplished without amending the UN Charter. Because of the criticality of the matter, I'll be quite detailed and specific.

A minority of the five Permanent Members should not have the right to prevent the Security Council from carrying out its primary function of maintaining the peace through implementation of Rule of Law; any Permanent Member of the Security Council which is a party to an issue under consideration should, in all fairness, recuse itself, refrain from voting, just as judges everywhere must do when impartial judgment does not seem possible. Employing such objectivity would gain enormous respect for the Permanent Five Members and allay legitimate concerns of the smaller nations. There is no *obligation* to vote or to exercise a veto; nations can, and often have, refrained voluntarily from doing so.

What's vitally needed in addition, though, is a means of assuring impartial 'judges.' No Perm Five Member should be allowed to be, simultaneously, an accused and a "judge" of the legality of its own behavior, such as, acting in violation of the UN Charter, Security Council Resolutions or other international law, in the instance—or aiding or abetting client states which are in such violations—or voting on its own misdeeds. These violations would include: the crime of aggression or a party thereto, or providing to other nations illicit weapons, such as chemical, biological or nuclear weapons, or the means for other nations to create such illicit weapons outlawed by binding treaties, or the means to deliver them, for example, by missile. It would be a mockery of justice if a Permanent Five rogue member were permitted to vote in such situations.

I will now outline approaches to remedy such misuse of the veto; the New Millennium Panel is now at work drafting the detailed curative measures. The first approach: the adoption by the Security Council of a procedural rule which would prevent such misuse of power by a Perm Five Member, or even two such Permanent Members acting in collaboration. In this connection the Charter specifically provides (Article 30) that "The Security Council shall adopt its own rules of procedure, including the method of selecting its President." And Article 27 provides that "Decisions of the Security Council on procedural matters shall be made by an affirmative vote of nine members" and "Decisions of the Security Council on all other matters shall be made by an affirmative vote of nine members including the votes of the permanent members" in certain matters in which "a party to a dispute shall abstain from voting." In sum, one—or two— Permanent Members perceived by the majority of the Security Council as an outlaw in the instance, its (or their) veto would not be recognized. By so interpreting Article 27 it would well make the difference between war or peace.

Also, the very fact of the existence of well-crafted, Charter-authorized rules of procedures to cover these situations should act to dissuade Permanent Members from violating Charter provisions or international law—in other words, to be "squeaky clean."

An alternate approach. Threaten to start proceedings to expel from the United Nations a rogue Permanent Five Member or, if necessary, proceed to do so. There are many requirements in the UN Charter which set standards for all UN members; Violation of any could be grounds for expulsion. These include:

- Fulfilling obligations assumed by them in accordance with the Charter.
- Settling international disputes by peaceful means.

- Refrain in their international relations from the threat or use of force against the territorial integrity or political independence of any state.
- All members shall give every assistance in any action it takes in accordance with the Charter, and shall refrain from giving assistance to any state against which the UN is taking preventive or enforcement action.

Likewise, there are other obligations upon becoming a member of the UN:

- To be peace-loving and able and willing to carry out its obligations.
- A member against which preventive and enforcement action has been taken by the Security Council may be suspended from the exercise and privileges of membership by the General Assembly upon recommendation by the Security Council.
- And, finally, a member of the UN which persists in violating the principles contained in the Charter may be expelled from the Organization of the General Assembly upon recommendation of the Security Council.

Within the above Charter provisions there exists plenty of leverage to make a rogue Member of the Security Council, including Permanent Members, comply on critical issues—by threatening expulsion—or proceeding to do so.

If worldwide Rule of Law is ever to be realized, hardball methods, such as compliance, or expulsion or the threat thereof, will be needed. Also, a Security Council Member, including a Permanent Member, could decide to resign from the United Nations over a crucial issue. Better that than one nation nullifying or forestalling the Security Council on a crucial issue, such as the forty-odd years of blocking the will of the Security Council in the Cold War, or dealing with another megalomaniac of the ilk of Tojo, Hitler or Stalin. Should it resign, it could find itself at odds with the entire world, and an array of impediments in its path. A dire step!

Worldwide Rule of Law is on the line. It's either worldwide Rule of Law together with its means of enforcement, or continue in the jungle. It will take a strong nation to lead the way forward.

I cannot overemphasize the importance of workable revised and fair procedures to make the Security Council truly effective. If this new procedural change or if the other remedies cited cannot be made effective for some reason, I believe the Security Council's ability to carry out its core mission of maintaining world peace will not be met and that, like the League of Nations, it will be unable to meet the challenges in matters of maintaining the peace and, thereby, thwarting the achievement of worldwide Rule of Law. On reflection, under this new veto-override procedure I believe that each law-abiding Permanent Five Member will see its own security increased—as well as the security of all nations.

In the near term our Ambassador to the United Nations will introduce the plan to the Security Council. I will inform you in advance.

At such time as the workable new Security Council veto override procedure comes into effect the United States will give full support to implementation of worldwide Rule of Law. There are several ways in which to proceed. It can make its share of forces available to the Security Council—to create the UN Peace Force that President Eisenhower proposed over forty years ago—fulfilling the Security Council's fifty-five-year-old Charter requirement to secure agreements with nations to provide quick reaction and follow-on forces. In agreements to that end, however, the United States will reserve its constitutional right to declare war, and to initiate combat. Also, it will reserve the right to approve command arrangements in advance of committing forces to any plan or situation. Needless to say, the United States will prepare backup plans to safeguard its vital interests.

Or, the Security Council can request a nation to prepare a multilateral plan for a particular contingency. Or, another alternative, advanced planning initiated by a single nation, but involving a number of nations, as was done by the United States for the

Gulf War. This latter alternative was the basis of the Security Council Resolutions which called for action against Iraq's invasion of Kuwait in 1991.

And, at an appropriate time, our Ambassador to the UN will propose to the Security Council the creation of a Combined Military Staff, replacing the existing—but unused—shell of a Military Staff Committee, thus enabling the preparation of broad-based multilateral—or combined force—planning designed to deter and defeat aggression and for other violations of international law and, as well, for peacekeeping. For lack of a military staff the Article 26 provision in the UN Charter, the "establishment of a system for the regulation of armaments," remains an obligation unfulfilled for over fifty years. And by default, for the lack of the military staff, Secretary-Generals have been obliged over the years to personally organize and oversee peacekeeping operations, taking up an inordinate amount of their time and attention.

The United States—and I trust other nations—will respond to Security Council requests to prepare contingency plans for the conduct of specific multilateral military peacemaking as well as peacekeeping operations. I believe that the fact of Security Council planning of any of these alternatives, done openly, with public knowledge, will act as a powerful deterrent to rogue-led nations.

As these steps fall into place the United States will discontinue apace its role of world policeman, thereby saving American lives and treasure. In any situation that I foresee requiring a military solution, there will be many nations with interests, thus calling for multilateral planning, action and forces.

As these forces will be enforcing Rule of Law on behalf of all law-abiding nations, it is appropriate and necessary that a system be established for reimbursement; I do not wish to repeat the reimbursement system the United States used in the Gulf War, wherein a few nations offset United States' costs of about $57 billion—making United States costs $7 billion—and thereby making our troops mercenaries. A balance in these situations is necessary.

And, much the same as President Bush's offer, the United States will make available a suitable military facility in the New York City area to accommodate the military staff and provide for conferencing and planning, as well as limited training.

I would like to set straight that the failures in Somalia and early Bosnia, organized as it was, operating directly under the Security Council, were caused primarily by the lack of a military staff to advise the Security Council and for lack of a proper chain of command. It would be akin to my organizing, deploying, and communicating with field commanders—without the Pentagon. As indicated previously, there are other ways available to organize such operations; each military operation requires a plan tailored to the specific situation.

Of critical importance, together with establishing Rule of Law, is the elimination of weapons of mass destruction. If it were not for a measure of rationality during the Cold War between the United States and the former Soviet Union, I would not be speaking tonight, this building might not exist, or possibly Washington itself might not exist. I refer, of course, to an exchange of nuclear weapons. The United States developed the nuclear weapon in order to end a savage war of aggression but, in the process, started the nuclear arms race. And this threat of annihilation has hung over us for decades. Although we may have the feeling of being more secure now that the Cold War is over, thousands of nuclear weapons still exist, usable almost instantly—and are, increasingly, in more hands. And even now weapons designers are visualizing weapons that would trivialize the thermonuclear weapon.

I am determined to find a way to bring the nuclear weapon era to a close, to enlist other nations to join in eliminating all weapons of mass destruction—as well as to outlaw and prevent the development of the very concept of any new such weapons. To be successful, of course, both rigid international inspection and verification are essential.

Now Russia and the United States continue to reduce nuclear weapons, but much too slowly. Also, the United States, Russia and other nations have the difficult and costly task, in addition to their dismantling and destruction, of cleaning up fissile material left from the frenzied making of the weapons. We continue to search for safer ways to do this cleanup job, as well as storing the fissile material. We will share any breakthroughs in this regard.

I will be proposing a series of conventions to speed up destruction of nuclear warheads, together with their delivery systems, and do it on a Fast Track—by Executive Order—as present reductions proceed at a snail's pace. The present system is agonizingly slow, whereas it is the rapidity of reduction that is paramount. The Senate, of course, will continue to ratify umbrella agreements or treaties, and I will keep Congress informed of the progress on them. I am sure that Congress will see the wisdom in expediting the process; early elimination is paramount.

First, I will propose to the President of Russia that we meet to establish a plan for setting a timetable for reduction to zero of nuclear weapons and missile defense systems, using Fast Track. I couple the two weapons systems, as they are inevitably interrelated. I will propose the de-alerting and pledges or agreements of "no first use" in the meanwhile. Also, I will propose to my counterpart that at appropriate stages the destruction of delivery systems in both of our countries be televised simultaneously worldwide in order that the entire world can witness the process, thus providing reassurance to our own people, as well as all nations, in particular the other nuclear nations.

Second, upon reaching agreement with Russia, I will propose to the President of Russia that we meet with the leaders of China, France, the United Kingdom and the other "have" nations, with a view of their producing, likewise, a timetable for the reduction of their nuclear warheads, their delivery and defense systems to reach zero coincident with the United States and Russia reaching zero. The worldwide televising of their destruction, likewise, would have salutary effects.

Third, under the same formula, I will propose that the Presidents of the United States and Russia meet early-on with the undeclared or potential nuclear weapons nations, including Iraq, Iran, Libya, Israel and North Korea, with the same agenda.

Fourth, at the propitious time I will propose a convention of the twenty-five-or-more nations which have or are working to acquire chemical and biological weapons, with a view to their destruction, as well as their delivery systems and manufacturing facilities.

The United Nations Special Committee (UNSCOM), which has done a commendable job in monitoring banned weapons in Iraq within its restraints, could be expanded and provided with new powers to meet inspection requirements under the new verification system.

Transparency will be the norm. All nations will have full knowledge of the overall plan in every step of its execution.

Many believe that reducing nuclear weapons to zero is not possible, arguing that there will be powerful incentives for nations to hide some as a contingency against hostile breakout.

For some time I have had in mind a plan that would not only facilitate the reaching of agreements for reducing nuclear weapons to zero but, also, would deal with any nation that manages to evade inspection and controls, to hide weapons—to cheat.

I envisage a force operating under the aegis of the Security Council, a World Prevention Force, to deal with such nations. I see the force as a number of uniquely marked ships or submarines, plying continuously the high seas on random courses, or aircraft strategically located around the world—or an appropriate mix of these forces—each with one or more long-range missiles appropriately armed as well as a missile defense capability, while maintaining readiness at all times. The Prevention Force mission: deter the use of weapons of mass destruction, to be prepared to destroy any launched missiles, and to be prepared to attack their source anywhere in the world. Already, I have assigned a panel the responsibility of determining the best mix and the modus operandi for the World Prevention Force.

I will coordinate with other potential participating nations prior to offering a plan to the Security Council, including, inter alia: establishment of clear command arrangements, clear Rules of Engagement, explicit control arrangements for the use of appropriate weapons, and remuneration by the UN for services rendered by the participants.

The combination of the United Nations Peace Force and the eliminating of nuclear weapons and missile defenses reinforce each other. The UN Peace Force, designed to deter aggression or in its instance nip aggression in the bud, the eliminating of nuclear weapons, backed up by the World Prevention Force—all three interacting and mutually supporting—add up to an infinitely more peaceful world. Timing is all-important. The Peace Force must be a truly effective deterrent force well in advance of the time the last nuclear weapons are destroyed; nations must feel secure before relinquishing their nuclear weapons. With all elements of both forces in place and fully operational, together with the verification of elimination, nations should, in fact, be far more secure. I propose the year 2020 as the target date for zeroing nuclear weapons and all other weapons of mass destruction. Thus, this inter-related, mutually supporting international strategy needs be started now, in this benign period.

In discussions with my advisors, I pointed out that we are looking twenty years into the future, that by then the concept of worldwide Rule of Law should be well established, that there should be a substantial decrease in the numbers of Security Council peacemaking as well as peacekeeping operations, conducted under one or more of the several options available. We explored and discussed thoroughly the issues involved: Rule of Law vs. rule of the jungle, that the role of the active, competent Peace Force is essential to world peace, just as are police forces within nations, and all the other elements involved. There was a consensus that all could be accomplished under the existing UN Charter. As an inveterate planner, I think it not only useful but indispensable that long range international planning be conducted to provide for world security. Nations have conducted long range security planning as a necessity, out of fear; it's time to start planning—and implementing—world peace together, based on law.

Tonight I offer this strategy to the community of nations, to be followed by specific proposals to all involved nations; at the appropriate time I will pursue the matters with the Security Council. I welcome your reactions.

My sensing is that at this stage of history national leaders have come to realize not only the apocalyptic consequences of the use of weapons of mass destruction but also the wasteful consequences of diverting resources from useful, productive ends, including the negative impact on economic viability, but most fundamentally the impact on people.

Breakthroughs are needed, also, to deal with new, ever more destructive weapons for deployment or employment, even in space, as well as to achieve an effective ban on concepts of new weapons of mass destruction. It makes utmost sense to me to avoid new arms races, to avoid repeating the likes of the United States—Soviet arms race or the creation of missile defenses, to avoid trying to out-build each other in creating enormous stockpiles of new weapons, then, having come to our senses, to destroy them. What a shocking waste. I am not one to wait for dire events to happen. To the utmost of my ability, I will act to prevent arms races.

Space warrants a special mention. Today, development of space is booming. It is now used for the handling of global communications for civilians, for weather information, navigation, for environmental management, television and many other constructive purposes. These and newer breakthroughs will make space even more critical to the modern world. Also, military forces increasingly make use of space for reconnaissance, for locating enemy forces, the guidance of weapons, and more. Some military leaders are proposing that weapons will be placed in space—in violation of international law—such as a space-based directed energy weapons which could do immense damage to a nation's warmaking capacity in a matter of hours, even minutes. Some say that the next war will be in space. To them, I say the United States will not only not initiate the placing of any weapons in space, but will act quickly to oppose others who plan to do so. There have been too many arms races already.

I have directed the Secretary of State with its Arms Control, Disarmament and Prevention function, in coordination with the Secretary of Defense, to develop a plan designed to prevent space from becoming an arena of international military competition and confrontation. In this connection, space law needs updating. For example, earth-orbiting weapons are prohibited, but stationary or earth based weapons targeting on space are not specifically addressed. I have directed that Arms Control, Disarmament and Prevention Agency be reconstituted within the State Department. And note that I have added "Prevention" to ACDA's responsibilities. I'll be referring to it as ACD&P Agency henceforth.

Our Ambassador to the United Nations will propose the establishment of a series of regional headquarters thereby facilitating United Nations peacemaking and peacekeeping operations, as well as other United Nations functions. Forces within the regions would be trained to assist in peacekeeping operations. He will propose Africa as the first in view of the turbulent situations in some areas there, with others in several areas to follow.

I am proposing the creation of a United Nations Global Security College under the Security Council for the study of the new ways and means of peacemaking, peacekeeping and prevention of conflict under international law.

Shocked by India's starting a nuclear arms race with its neighbor Pakistan, a race that forebode dire prospects for the entire area, I am directing our Ambassador to the United Nations to introduce to the Security Council a plan designed to prevent similar future conduct in the world. In a nutshell, it will propose that, when two or more nations become involved in a dispute having the potential of breaking the peace, the Security Council will form a Watch Group of representatives of two or more nations to investigate, report to the Security Council, and initiate whatever action is required, to include arbitration, mediation or other appropriate measures.

As currently individual nations, including our own, focus on such situations only spasmodically, the Watch Group would maintain a presence, remaining in constant touch until a remedy is found. Successful use of this technique could reduce significantly the number of peacekeeping operations required, as well as peace-making operations.

In this same vein I am directing our Ambassador to introduce a plan to deal with nations identified as rogue-led nations. This plan will involve diplomatic approaches designed to bring them into the community of nations as well as for remedial action in the event that such nations violate international law or norms.

Under the many new policies and in view of anticipated increase in national security activity, I will streamline systems and procedures in the Executive Branch. I will look to both the Secretaries of Defense and State—with its the extremely important Arms Control, Disarma-ment and Prevention Agency—for the security of our nation, Defense, in the traditional way, and State/ACD&P Agency, through an ener-gized arms reduction and preventive program, as well as through diplomacy. I intend that they be closely coordinated so that arms re-duction and prevention actions will not be impeded while, at the same time, our national security is preserved—resulting in a more balanced, effective, prosperous, and safer America. As a specific example, the two departments will coordinate on the development and testing of any new weapons systems which could possibly trigger an arms race or impede arms reduction measures. I will decide any differences.

A case in point is the deployment of a national missile defense system. I have placed missile defense on hold. My general policy is that solving international problems with military hardware will be of last resort, that all other means will be exhausted before the resort to hardware. This world has seen enough of arms races. Our offensive nuclear missile capability will act as a powerful deterrent—as has been made abundantly clear to all nations with a capability.

State/ACD&P Agency will be arranging a conference with all nations capable of building or operating missiles and missile de-fenses with the view of obtaining a worldwide Anti-Ballistic Treaty outlawing them. The overall objective: a world devoid not only of missile defenses but of missiles, nuclear weapons, as well as all weapons of mass destruction.

I have charged my National Security Advisor to be in close touch with State and Defense at all times to assure implementation of this policy and to keep me fully informed.

Furthermore, I am establishing a permanent Coordination Group, which will not only coordinate the formulation of the many new policies involved in the New Strategy for America but, as well, the implementing actions—in normal times as well as in crises. The Coordination Group will be headed by my National Security advisor and comprised of senior individuals seconded to the heads of the White House staff, the Department of State/ACD&P Agency, CIA, FBI and the Atomic Energy Commission.

Also, I have charged the State Department, assisted by the CIA and FBI and supported by the Department of Defense, to head the development of a plan for dealing with the surreptitious introduction into the United States of all types of mass destruction weapons. When this subject comes up my thoughts go back to the World Trade Building bombing in New York. Its perpetrators' intent was to collapse both of its towers. Thank God they failed. In this connection I observe that implementation of worldwide Rule of Law would act to defuse the ire of rogue leaders against an individual nation, as they would be dealing with the community of nations.

Further, I have directed the CIA to cease activities involving the overthrow of a head of state. The United States would be aghast if such actions were taken against any high official in our government. Such activities have no place in a world under Rule of Law; they become matters of interest to the nations of the community of nations—not the old, outdated, 'us' vs. 'them,' but of the new, 'law abiding' vs. 'outlaws and outlaw nations.'

In this connection, I have formed a high level, ad hoc board to review the CIA's role in light of the New Strategy for America and to make recommendations to me as to its new role.

In retrospect, the bombing of a rogue's training camp in Afghanistan and a chemical plant in Sudan in retaliation for the bombing of two US Embassies in Africa only intensified bin Laden's hatred for the US, whereas his enemies included Jews and Catholics, besides America. Yes, we retaliated instantly against a movement that hated many, but again the US acted as a self-appointed policeman, resulting in intensified hatred against the US and the ire of Sudan's and Afghanistan's leaders. It's a fine line as to whether the US acted lawfully, in self-defense, or as a rogue nation; there are at least two nations which thought the latter. And months later there was still no clear evidence that the chemical plant in Sudan was, in fact, manufacturing nerve gas.

A better course, under Rule of Law, would have been to provide the Security Council with a plan to throttle rogue bin Laden, including the attacking of his sites. Belatedly, the US placing a bounty on his head was a useful step—and should have been the initial and only step. The US seems to want instant gratification, but in the process exacerbating a rogues' ire, thus compounding the problem, just as arms races only compound the problem. World security problems should—and can only be—solved by community action. Should the Security Council fail to act, then is the time to weigh taking unilateral action.

In view of the many facets involved in the paramount mission of preventing armed conflict I have charged the Secretary of State with the lead role in the executive branch of formulating related policy and, as well, advising me as to initiatives for new weapons systems which could precipitate new arms races.

A word to the members of Congress. Needless to say, the support of Congress is crucial to the implementation of the New Strategy for America, as is the support of the American people. As I alluded earlier, the American people subscribe to all the main tenets of this New Strategy for America. Polls show that they have a favorable opinion of the United Nations. A high percentage want the United States to pull back from its role of world policeman and want the rest of the world to bear more of the burden. A very high percentage support the creation of United Nations standby and ready reaction forces; a high percentage favor the idea of United Nations peacekeeping operations; a majority favor allowing United States troops to execute United Nations Resolutions under certain circumstances; a very high percentage of Americans believe we should not go our own way in international affairs; and, Americans strongly favor eliminating nuclear weapons by balanced and verifiable agreements.

I believe we must not only respect their desires, but act on them. I, too, have held these views for a long time.

I have made a point of reviewing the matter of command and control and employment of our military forces. Knowing Congress' sensitivity in this regard I assure the Congress that any agreements made with the UN Security Council will meet our requirements. As all know, the President is always in command of United States troops. Should placing some of our troops under the operational control of another commander be appropriate, as has been the case for years in NATO planning, each situation will be reviewed with the greatest of care. Neither I nor, I'm sure, the Congress will permit the squandering of American lives.

The issue of sovereignty comes up frequently. I simply point out that every treaty, every convention, every agreement made with other nations impacts our sovereignty. We enter these because we see not only the United States benefited, but all the parties involved. The United States became a member of the United Nations for this reason. Because of our viable economy, our implementation of Rule of Law at home, and our military strength, the United States is in a unique position to exercise a leadership role in the United Nations. Put simplistically, either we work together on this planet or we continue in the jungle.

In the long run I believe firmly that implementation of this New Strategy for America will reduce the loss of American lives and treasure and will continue to decline as multilateral policing of the world is perfected, as violence subsides, as weapons of mass destruction are harnessed and destroyed. Virtually all nations will

benefit. I believe firmly, too, that a quieter, saner world will be reflected in the acts of Americans, thereby reducing acts of violence
in America.

I request that Congress pass a resolution supporting the New
Strategy for America, which would clear the air and weld together
Americans in what I believe is the most important peacetime en-
deavor in our history. As Congress is neither authorized nor equipped
to implement broad strategies such as this, I ask for its full support
in helping to carry it out. Then, both the White House and the Congress will be obligated to the American people to see the New Strategy for America through.

Currently, Congress tends to micromanage; it proceeds in jerks
and starts, taking issue with and often delaying vital elements of
our national security—such as in arms reduction treaties—in large
measure due to the fact that current strategy is ill-defined, and not
cohesive. Consensus on the new strategy should eliminate much
confusion and would present a united United States.

United Nations operations currently are hampered because of
the shortage of funds. It is in need of its legitimate dues. Paying our
arrears is in keeping with the New Strategy for America. Our minimal contribution of troops for peacekeeping alone warrants paying
our arrears in full.

I am well aware that many members of the Congress are disen-
chanted—to say the least—with the United Nations for its bureau-
cracy and inefficiency, but I would offer that many Americans think
much the same of the Congress. I point out that the United States
government has been working to fine-tune itself for more than four
times longer than the United Nations has been in existence. Many in
Congress are dismayed with the Security Council; both institutions
have raging debates and disagreements. No one nation can hold sway
on all issues at all times in the Security Council. Similarly, neither
political party in the Congress can hold sway on all issues, even
when it has a majority in both houses of Congress. We witness these
disagreements frequently, and note that some continue for years,

such as campaign financing, or reducing our onerous, long-standing national debt created mainly from wars or the preparation for war, now down to $3.7 trillion. Without enlightened compromise in both bodies, neither the Security Council nor our nation will progress, or move forward.

I expect the Senate to ratify the International Criminal Court Statute, designed to bring to justice those who are responsible for initiating wars of aggression, crimes against humanity, and other war crimes. Any nation authorized to enforce international law or operating within the law should not be concerned as to its application. The United States, especially, should be the example of lawful conduct, without which it cannot exercise a world leadership role. Further, I see this treaty as providing a great deterrent to rogue leaders. It codifies the Nuremberg trial precepts and fills the void in law which has inhibited the apprehension and trial of war criminals. Its purpose meshes well with The Strategy for America.

Neither I nor the members of Congress can know how successful the New Strategy for America will be—the mutually supporting elements of forestalling aggression and the taming, prevention and elimination of weapons of mass destruction, and the many other endeavours—but I am driven to do my utmost to fulfill Americans' aspirations, the promise of creating a more peaceful world. We remain in the jungle if we fail.

I have every confidence that the results of polls of Americans taken following my address tonight will help confirm and solidify the views of Americans. I look forward, also, to the views on this strategy from nations around the world.

There is need to move apace. For, based on the frequency of our wars this century—from the first to the last—our next war is due in the year 2007—unless preventive action is taken. Recall that none of these wars was anticipated. Now, no nation threatens seriously the security of the United States. And now, in this benign period, is the time to shift gears—after several million years in the jungle—to start anew by implementing fully worldwide Rule of Law.

Although I haven't spent time tonight on armed violence within nations, I visualize that with the creation of the Security Council Combined Military Staff, and the creation of regional headquarters and other refinements, that, also, there will be a significant reduction in the need for peacekeeping operations.

Needless to say, it will take time for all the pieces of the strategy to fall into place, just as nations continue to improve their efficiency and effectiveness. The United States has been working for over 200 years to fulfill the promise of its Constitution—and we continue to do so, stumbling occasionally but usually seeing the light. Yes, we have our own inefficiencies and, at times, do squander the American people's money and, most unfortunately, their lives.

I visualize the day when worldwide Rule of Law—together with the deterrent, preventive, and enforcement mechanisms in this strategy—becomes effective that rogue leaders will look to peaceful ways to conduct their affairs, that the term "rogue leaders" will fall into disuse, that they will become a dying breed, that they will realize that peaceful pursuits pay. The United States will offer its cooperation and help to rogue leaders to make the transition. Megalomaniacs, though hopefully deterred by the measures instituted, will continue to bend only to force.

I expect that this new strategy will not only serve United States' vital interests as well as the vital interests of all law-abiding nations, and will reduce increasingly the resort to war and its casualties and, that by nipping aggression in the bud, another world war can be averted, that resources now devoted to war can be diverted to constructive ends, that nations will not only be more secure but will also feel secure, thus reducing the need for defensive weapons.

All will find a different United States, which will conduct its foreign affairs in a fundamentally new way befitting worldwide Rule of Law, a United States which is ready and willing not only to engage with any nation—to discuss any matters or issue at any time— but also willing to cooperate, to compromise, to come to terms, to reach genuine accommodation, and to assist in any way feasible. We will take care if other nations have an interest in a situation or are involved in an instant issue, that before intervening, the United States will consult with them in advance.

I enjoin all nations to support actively these vital changes in the world. All will gain. Each will have the same stature and rights under Rule of Law; all can appeal injustices against them. Under Rule of Law all law-abiding nations will find their relationships changed significantly for the better in many ways.

I truly believe that perfecting the enforcement of worldwide Rule of Law will be celebrated centuries hence as being a prominent milestone in the advancement of the human species.

I thank you. Good night. Sleep well.